Benjamin
Perkins

The Enchanted Garden

Discovering & Enhancing the Magical
Healing Properties in your Garden

CLAIRE O'RUSH

Trafalgar Square Publishing

First published in the United States of America in 1996 by
Trafalgar Square Publishing, North Pomfret, Vermont 05053

Printed and bound in Dubai, United Arab Emirates

Library of Congress Catalog Card Number: 96–60072

ISBN: 1–57076–057–8

Produced and designed by
SAVITRI BOOKS LTD
115J Cleveland Street
London W1P 5PN

Art direction and design by Mrinalini Srivastava
Edited by Caroline Taggart

Photography by Curtis, Lane & Co, Sudbury, Suffolk
Typeset in Galliard by Type Technique, London W1
Color origination by Regent Publishing Services Ltd, Hong Kong
Printed and bound by Oriental Press Ltd, United Arab Emirates

IMPORTANT NOTICE

Plants are very powerful healing tools. If they are misused, they can be harmful. The
natural remedies contained in this book are safe if used as directed, however, neither
the author, the producers nor the publishers of this book can be held responsible for
any adverse reactions to the recipes, formulas or recommendations contained herein.
Before trying any herbal formula, sample a small quantity first in case you have any
adverse or allergic reaction. Do not try self-diagnosis or attempt self-treatment for
serious or long term problems without consulting a qualified medical herbalist.
Do not take herbal remedies if you are undergoing any other course of medical
treatment without seeking professional advice.

Contents

The Enchanted Garden
is for Simon Rippon,
who inspired it.

Introduction

Paradise, Eden, Mother Earth . . . we are told all these are or were once gardens, although the Earth is now badly scarred because of our greed and ignorance. But perhaps there is a way of synthesizing all three, from the concept of perfection we call Paradise, down to Heaven on Earth, which was Eden, through at last to the New Age vision that our planet is a precious garden, encompassing wilderness and cultivated ground in its stately reaches; a way of healing the planet, ourselves and others through the creation of our own enchanted garden.

However simple and humble our individual plot may be, we can seek the deeper understanding that will enable us to create a microcosm to reflect the macrocosm. To be a gardener on any level is to have a sacred vocation, yet we have to move away from mundane and materialistic concepts if we are to enter the world of enchantments, miracles and wonders which is our true destiny. This does not mean, of course, that we can afford to forget about practical issues. It is more a matter of earthing the divine than of moving away from the Earth.

Yet we do need to leave limitation and fear of the imagination behind, and begin to realize that what we perceive with our inner, heart-centred senses is a picture of truth. Only then will we emancipate that truth so that it can be given free expression and manifestation in our world, becoming real for us first of all in the world of the garden. Such a garden can then become a focal point where our spiritual and earthly lives merge.

When I began to write *The Enchanted Garden* I thought of choosing my illustrations largely from the paintings of the Pre-Raphaelites. Their prevailing mood echoes my purpose in that they express through symbols and spiritual vision the atmosphere of the awakened soul, whose sublimities must be tapped so that the habitual sense of the mundane and the everyday can recede and begin to be subsumed by one of mystery and wonder. The work of the Pre-Raphaelite Brotherhood seeks out the mysticism, the soul manifestations, of Nature and her sisterhood with the human soul. Then I discovered that one of the lesser known artists of the Brotherhood, John Waterhouse, had died leaving his last painting unfinished. It was called *The Enchanted Garden.* This happy coincidence set the seal on my intention.

I believe that the philosophy of Romanticism, of seeking within for truth, is rightly applied to the contemplation of trees and flowers, of wild meadows and tended lawns, and that the mystery of Nature breathes through these paintings and gives them their secret force.

NOTE ON THE TEXT

In preparing this book I have occasionally drawn from the words and wisdom of my great-grandmother Sarah Greaves, a Victorian wisewoman from my native Yorkshire, and would like to acknowledge my indebtedness to the inspiration of her spirit.

Claire O'Rush, April 1996

The True Story of Anne Jefferies, related by Moses Pitt, 1696. In the year 1645, she then being nineteen years old, she being one day knitting in an arbour in our garden, there came over the garden hedge to her, as she affirmed, six persons, of a small stature, all clothed in green, which she called fairies; upon which, she was so frighted, that she fell into a kind of convulsion-fit . . . On her recovery, she begins to work miracles and by the blessing of God, cures her old mistress's leg, which had been hurt by a fall as she was coming from the mill . . . From Morgan's *Phoenix Brittanicus,* 1732

The Angel of the Garden

There is an angel in your garden. If you tend a plot of ground with love and care, no matter how small it may be, you invoke the presence of the Angel of the Garden. It is possible to form a bond of conscious communion with the Angel, a communion which stems from and is received in the heart. Because of this natural unfolding of spiritual perception, it is well to create a corner of privacy in the garden, even if you do no more than to establish one of the rustic bowers which can be purchased nowadays. Such a sequestered nook, however tiny, enables us to open a window on to the sublime sweetness of the angelic worlds with all their peace and wisdom and visionary inspiration informed by the spirit of love.

Who is this mysterious angel? What is her place in the hierarchy of the angelic host?

The angel who cares for our own individual garden (and there are as many angels as there are gardens) is one of the countless hosts of beings working under the direction of the great Earth Angel, one of the four mighty Angels of the Elements, that great cross of interacting matter which holds our physical existence together.

Although her ministrations are concerned with the Earth, the Earth Angel is spiritually associated with Venus, planet of love, harmony, beauty and art, which is so closely allied to our evolution here on Earth. Much that is good and beautiful comes to us from the heart of Venus and her exquisite angels and spirits, who are the bearers of divine love. Over them watches and presides the Great Goddess of all, the mother aspect of the Godhead, who pours her spirit into the Goddess of Venus and the Earth Goddess herself. It is these beings, under the direction of the Great Mother, that the Earth

The Blessed Damozel (detail), Dante Gabriel Rossetti, 1828-82

Angel embraces, channelling their love, their divinity, their mothering spirit, into the forms of Nature and physical being, incorporating all the four elements, because there is loving and mystic co-operation and communion between the Mighty Four.

Within the cosmic robes of the Earth Angel, beautiful and vast beyond even the enchanted imagination, the lesser angels, the fairies and Nature spirits dance and move and have their being. As we attune our sensitivity to the loveliness and the peace of our garden, we can begin to comprehend these mystic robes, perhaps even to perceive them with inner sight. It is within them that our own Angel of the Garden has her existence; she in turn directs the nobler fairies and Nature spirits, the graceful and laughing elves and the numerous hordes of tiny fairy beings who swarm in and among the flowers, administering their thousand services.

These robes of the Earth Angel which radiate from her essence and play upon the Earth are the spiritual substance out of which Divine Intelligence creates the miracle of physical form. The Earth Angel directs her host of exuberantly joyful workers from the fairy, elemental and spirit kingdoms to build form with physical matter; and so that form can continue always to evolve, these workers weave the pattern of cycles into matter, the great cycles of birth, death and rebirth which release it from form and enable a new cycle to begin. With each revolution these spiralling cycles express more perfectly the ideal which initiated its own expression in living matter; and so the evolutionary forces of our garden-planet Earth are ever building a 'stairway to Heaven'. All Nature is under the care of the ministering Earth Angel; and when we create a garden and seek spiritual sanctuary within it, the Angel of the Garden is able to channel our efforts so that they serve the Earth Angel and, through her, the great plan for humanity in the coming age.

To commune with the Angel of the Garden we need to be still, gently to refuse all distractive thoughts, to seek the point of quietude and spiritual power which lies within the heart. We need to centre our awareness on the heart as the focal point of our consciousness. Then, in the silence, in the stillness within, we will begin to hear the voice of the Angel of the Garden.

Buddleia and Japanese Anemones, Benjamin Perkins

Angelic Blessings

It is important to think of the Angel of the Garden very often in our musings and meditations from day to day, not merely as a whimsical notion or as a romantic ideal, but rather as a transforming truth, an absolute reality grounded in the actual as is the material world which surrounds us. The verities teach that the sphere of matter is illusory, ever shape-shifting with the passage of time, whereas the angelic worlds are brilliant with the principle of eternity, free from death and decay and constantly and steadfastly with us, if we choose to throw open the door which leads to them.

Sometimes the pressures and burdens of life press in upon us with great clamour, and it is not easy to still the mind and to silence niggling thoughts, which is an essential process when we wish to contact the Angel of the Garden. On such occasions it is helpful to start by perambulating the perimeters of the garden, carrying clearly within the mind the intent to commune with the soul of the garden. It is this soul which the Angel is building from the material you offer her, and which comes under her care and protection.

Begin by taking measured and steady steps and, if you can, walk to the sound of some music which inspires you. It is better to walk clockwise, and of course you can circle the garden as many times as you wish before coming to rest. We can bring a vivid and brilliant light which is yet consummately gentle and peaceful down from the spiritual worlds as we perambulate the garden. This light is the essence, the spiritual substance of wholeness, and it is a light which heals. We absorb this light through the breath, for, as we are taught by the mystery schools spanning the ages, human breath is magical.

The Annunciation (detail), Edward Reginald Frampton,
1872-1923

But we cannot realize this power of the breath unless we breathe 'through the heart'. This means that we should focus upon the breath intake so that we draw it right into the heart, more slowly than usual, yet gently and deeply. There should be nothing laboured or forced about this process. As the breath enters the heart, we consciously draw the light down from the spiritual realms, from Heaven or Paradise if we prefer to think of them as such. The magical light, white and golden in hue, will fill our entire being and we can now, in a conscious act of will, breathe it out to bless and heal the garden. This magical act of summoning and giving out the light can be used to heal any negative condition in life. It can even be sent out consciously by the individual to heal the nations and our Mother Earth, or to heal an absent friend. Yet a natural and simple way to practise this is first to bring down the light into the garden, where the magical effects of its nurturing will soon become visible.

A deeply meaningful symbol to use when embarking upon this walk is that of a six-pointed star, shining pure and clear in the heavens (without the divisions of the traditional Star of David). Our own hearts vibrate in symphony with the heart of this beautiful star shining with the exquisite brilliance of Paradise, which is the light of love.

As you place each step upon the ground, remember that walking is a sacred act, and that the earth beneath your feet is holy. This will help to stimulate a cherishing stream of love to flow forth from the heart as a wave of light, of actual spiritual substance. It is possible mentally to direct this spiritual substance of love from our hearts where it is received into the feet so that each footstep can sow the light deep into the ground. As the light from your heart, from your breathing, permeates the soil, feel the divine light which is secreted in the heart of the Earth leap up joyfully and, using you as its conductor, offer itself in adoration of the light coming down from the spiritual spheres. Thus, you yourself become a channel, a magical vehicle, for the mystical communion of Earth and Heaven. When this communion takes place, the Earth Angel is able to lift our planet a little further up her 'stairway to Heaven'. Yet this grand cosmic process begins with us, in our own back garden, as we enter into natural communion with our deepest heart, aided and fostered in every way by the beautiful and simple service of our Angel of the Garden, who is always present when we raise our consciousness above the mundane and the commonplace as we enter the garden.

When the perambulation of the garden has been completed, sit down and become very still in mind and body. Continue breathing 'through the heart' and quietly call upon the Angel of the Garden. Ask her to speak with you. Ask that you may come into her presence. After you have experienced the joy of this communion for a while, you can begin to put practical requests to the Angel, asking her help in blessing, healing and revitalizing the garden. You can ask for inspiration for building harmony and loveliness into the flowers and trees, for creating focal points of beauty which will give a sense of sanctuary. If you have a desire to create bowers and arbours, after building (or purchasing) the necessary structures and deciding upon the vines and trees with which you feel most in harmony, give the Angel a mind picture of how you wish the finished effect to look, and then encourage and talk to the plants so that they will sculpt themselves according to your vision. If you follow these instructions regularly, in heightened consciousness, you will begin to witness many little miracles, offered quietly from the heart of the Angel of the Garden and the Nature beings who co-operate with her.

MEDITATION FOR LISTENING AND SPEAKING TO THE ANGEL OF THE GARDEN

First of all, envision a golden rose blooming in glory at your heart centre. Focus calmly and peacefully upon this perfect golden rose, breathing gently and slowly. Make yourself small enough to nestle in the heart of the rose, deep amongst its petals. Now you are as a tiny child in the presence of the Angel, centred entirely in your heart consciousness, that mind in the heart which is the true guide and teacher of humanity. Speak the words of this invocation:

Angel of the Garden, still my waiting soul, so my eyes may see your radiance, my spirit enter into your peace, as your wings unfold to gather this place of tended growing things into your heart. I feel the breath of the Angel as a gentle incense moving through the airs which play upon this garden. I feel the touch of the Angel as each blade of grass, each sprig, flower, herb and tree, each living creature, is blessed. I hear the song of the Angel as each plant moves and dances, with a motion unseen, to the perfect harmony of the spheres. The life of the spirit walks in my garden as an angel, and my garden is made holy, a place of benediction. The Angel of the Garden hears my prayer, and draws near. In reverence I bow to the Angel, and give my heart and hands into the light of her inspiration.

Create the images contained within the meditation easily, without stress or struggle. Imagination is our key to the door which opens on to a higher reality, but the process needs to be relaxed and flowing.

On completion of the invocation, after sitting quietly for some moments, begin to speak to the Angel directly, asking her advice and putting questions to her; or you may prefer to sit in quiescent contemplation. Whichever is the case, open your heart and listen, for you must be ready to receive the gifts of inspiration and renewal she will bring to you.

After the meditation, it is important to earth yourself before engaging in practical activities again. Do this by thinking of a silver cross in a ring of bright light and placing it as a protective seal upon your brow, throat and solar plexus centres.

MAGIC CASEMENTS

Some thousands of years ago, and continuing in intensity ever since, we offended the fairies and elementals, the spirits of woods and forests, of lakes and pools, the noble elves and fay folk of the wilderness, of the distant reaches of the ocean and the fastnesses of the hills and mountains, and instigated a war which rages to this day. That is one reason for the countless accidents and natural disasters of our history and of the present era, and for the numerous spells and charms to protect against malignant fairy magic. Yet if we would only allow our consciousness to embrace the fairy folk, and begin to learn from them, to respect and love them once again, our lives would be transformed and many of the problems and burdens which beset suffering humanity would be swiftly solved.

It is our destiny to recognize our brotherhood with the fairies, and to work together on the Earth plane to create nourishment for our bodies and souls, true nourishment which will not deplete Mother Earth, but which will offer an equal measure of nurturing and well-being to her in return for her free-handed gifts.

Bluebells, Benjamin Perkins

One of the most meaningful, beautiful and simple lessons that the fairies can teach us is how to sing forth a note of profound joy in our daily life as we fulfil our round of duties. This will lift the drudgery and sense of burden from them and liberate us into spiritual realms of freedom, because when we face necessity in a spirit of joy and enthusiasm, we can challenge its limitations and transform and transcend them. This note of bubbling joy, exuberance and good-willed humour is the magical sound of vibration of the ray upon which the fairies have their being, and we can learn from them how to sound it forth from our hearts.

There are levels of life which are intensely beautiful, rewarding and fulfilling if only we could remember how to gain access to them. The fairies will teach us to take the first step by obviating the need for those unwise stimulants which draw from abysmal astral levels, and which exist to degrade and enslave humanity. When we learn from the fairies to feed our souls on a sense of liberation, exhilaration and enjoyment which arises from simple and natural pleasures, the way to attainment of these higher realms will begin to clear before us.

Here is a simple exercise to help us begin to aspire to this lesson, using the garden as our place of study.

EXERCISE TO EXPERIENCE THE FAIRY JOY

Go out at daybreak, just before sunrise, and attune yourself to the fairy life in the garden by becoming still and opening the heart centre; give out a call of greeting silently from the heart, saluting the fairy folk with love and respect. As the sun begins to rise, an overwhelming surge of childlike joy will wash over you, bringing in its wake the ardent *gaiety* of the fairies, full of the artless embrace of happiness which makes little children hop, skip and run of necessity. The feeling is akin to that of a child when it wakes on Christmas morning, or on the first day of the summer holidays, and needs to be remembered. Bathe in the sparkling colours of this feeling and store it safely in memory, because then you will find that you are able to summon it again at will. This is the Joy of the Fairies, and it is their precious gift to humanity, if only we will heed and accept it.

Ophelia, John William Waterhouse, 1849-1917

There are many kinds of fairies at work in the world, and to attract them into our garden we have to learn to pour love into its heart, so that we cherish every living thing within its precincts. Even those insects and animals we would discourage need to be thanked for playing their part in Nature's cycle before they are humanely banished. This approach will draw us closer to the fairies.

Fairies cannot bear us to turn our gaze directly upon them, as our present state of consciousness is too much of an abomination. So we have to learn to catch a glimpse of them from the corners of our eyes, discreetly and cautiously, as if they were timid wild creatures going about their business unaware that we have noticed them. The fairies cannot be fooled, of course. They are aware that we are trying to observe them. Yet in spite of their reservations they are infinitely curious about the human race and are ready to love us and work with us, if we prove ourselves to be worthy of their co-operation.

The fairies exist on a hierarchical scale, as do the angels. The tiniest and the simplest of these magical beings are the swarms of minuscule fairies whose work is to attend to the day-to-day requirements of each and every plant. The life-cycle of the plant is facilitated by these numerous fairies, perfect in form and beautiful to behold; yet their awareness is limited, and when their work is completed, they die naturally with their plant, like a leaf in the winds of autumn. Their essence returns to their Angel, for they comprise the objectification of her energies, at work on the Earth plane.

Then there are the flower fairies and the wood elves, the brownies, imps, goblins and sprites, which vivify and foster the forces and energies of Nature, stimulating the field of energy in a wood or a meadow or a garden, or perhaps on some wild stretch of moorland or mountainside. They minister to individual flowers as well, bringing to them their life essence so that they shine with the radiant hue of the Nature spirit who attends them. The work of these taller fairies is in some respects similar to the duties of the tiny fairies, only at a more advanced and subtle level. They are individualized, and possess their own unique consciousness and awareness. Margaret Tarrant and Cicely Mary Barker are two of a number of artists who clearly saw the etheric forms of the fairy folk and who faithfully reproduced them in their drawings and paintings. The flower fairies are delicately exquisite in form and supremely lovely to look upon, reflecting like perfect jewels every colour of the rainbow, every variance of shade, and some colours that the material world is too gross to be able to express, and for which we have no name. Yet they can make themselves appear grotesque and repellently ugly (rather like some of the forms Arthur Rackham intuited in his art).

Finally, there exist the truly noble fays, those beings who live within the etheric substance of matter, which enables them to dwell inside mountains and rocks, hills and mounds, and also underground. Although all fairy beings exist within the etheric substance of their own element, these are the fairy worlds, the true Fairyland. Herein are to be found palaces, halls, countries, beautiful and wild terrain, enchanted seas and verdant landscapes of unsurpassed beauty. These mysterious fairy kingdoms are not entirely safe for mortals to wander in, as we are not yet ready to become cognizant of the forces, powers and knowledge that the inhabitants of these worlds wield.

These fairies, or more appropriately 'fays', are as tall as members of the human race, and some are considerably taller. They possess, like all the fairies, the power to change their height and shape at will, and it is true that they can contract their astral molecules to such a degree that they are able to float through keyholes! They delight in playing with the etheric forces at their command, and their pranks are often mistaken for the more sinister presence of ghosts or poltergeists.

The fays have their own profound, beautiful and evolved culture, and their music, song and dance are sights and sounds unforgettable once experienced. Many of the melodies in our folk music and in our classical repertoire were gifts of the fairies. Creative works of literature which penetrate the mysteries of life are not written without the granting of fairy insights, and grand balls held throughout history were and are based on the ceremonial rites of the fairies and elves as they dance in formation to create a palpable ball of golden energy which is directed into the essence of trees, grass and plants for their renewal and vivification.

The fays, and the lesser fairies, enjoy a certain pattern of family life, and fairy mothers nurture babies, as in human life. The fairy essence comes to Earth in the form of raindrops, snow crystals, sunbeams and moonbeams. According to its Angel, a number of these atoms are blessed in their higher etheric pattern. These Angel-kissed atoms, impregnated with fairy essence, gradually develop into a fairy being by attaching themselves to a plant.

The fays, like all fairies, are profoundly influenced and inspired by human beings. They, like us, are creatures who have sprung from the light seeds which are continually being broadcast into the universe by the spiritual sun operating through its physical counterpart, our own day star. The light seed which creates human individuals pulsates in the heart centre, the true point of consciousness. This light seed is a gift given to us – it is our 'own' seed atom and will remain so forever, giving each member of the human race the marvellous heritage of the gradual individuation into a son or daughter of the Godhead.

For the fays it is a little different – they are created from the undifferentiated essence of the light seed, and while they are individuals in their own right they are not so in the same sense as we are. When the higher fairies come to the end of their life-cycle, they do not die, but eventually evolve into angels or the mightier Nature spirits who have charge over planetary systems, but even at this elevated stage they are bound by spiritual laws which they cannot break. We have been given free will and can and do break spiritual law, and this is the subtle but boundlessly significant difference.

And so the fays are drawn to us, potential wonders of creation as we are, and they adopt our language, our ways, our ceremonies and customs, while simultaneously preserving their own magical culture. Some of the evolved fays even channel the incarnating fairy babies into their own etheric bodies and give birth in similar vein to human mothers. At the same time, the fairies are proud and sensitive beings, and mortal folk who lack respect in their dealings with them run the risk of falling under the fairy blight, which takes the form of diverse illnesses and incurable conditions.

A word should be said, perhaps, about negative elementals. These serve the darkness of life and it is wise not to dwell on them or to give them mental airspace. They are 'evil' in so far as we understand the term, but their harmfulness can be obviated by holding ourselves at the centre of a cross of light within a circle of light and bestowing a blessing of love and goodwill upon the creature that would hurt us, should we ever be hapless enough to encounter one of these unprepossessing entities!

What of the fairies in our garden? They will comprise the tiny hordes of fairies, the flower fairies and the wood elves, and perhaps

Green Hellebore, Benjamin Perkins

even, in time, the noble and gracious fays, if we are lucky. We need have no worries about mischievous sprites or negative elementals, because regular and faithful communion with the Angel of the Garden will soothe the former and banish the latter.

Words of advice on how to contact fairies and begin to see them are given in the manuscripts of Sarah Greaves:

> Look deep into the lovely forms of the flowers and the trees you care for and you will see the essence of their spirit dance and play as a rarefied white flame within their bodily form. This is the love and laughter of the Goddess as she smiles upon the Earth, giving charge to her angels and fairies to vivify and create all Nature anew . . .
>
> To open your heart to the fairies, you must nurture feelings of wonder, reverence and love for every detail of your garden, for the airs which blow about it, the musical rain which falls gently upon it, the high-riding storms which cause its spirit to resonate with the mighty spirits of the elements, the moon and the stars which silently look down on it, the great sun which is the source of its being, and for the clouds and the changing skies which provide it with a canopy. When you can truly feel the sweetness of this magic, you will begin to discover the fairies, for they will make themselves known to you.

A meditation for seeing and talking with the fairies follows, but remember that when working with any meditation or spell which concerns fairies or Nature spirits, it is always beneficial to sit quietly, as previously described, and seek contact first with the Angel of the Garden. Ask her to attune your heart to the wild heart of Nature. Begin to breathe 'through the heart' so that white light from this divine crucible flows from the source above, which is the star, down through you as its conductor, and right into the Earth below your feet, so that you are truly rooted in. You are now as a Tree of Light, with your roots in the Earth and your consciousness extending to the heavens.

Ask the Angel to accompany you, and pray that you might set out on a journey to meet the fairy people. Select one of Nature's forms nearby, close enough to contemplate with ease, and begin gently and

The Annunciation, Arthur Hughes, 1832-1915

easily to imagine the blessed white flame, the 'love and laughter of the Goddess', as it rises and plays in sacred dance within the physical sheath of the tree, plant or flower upon which you are focusing. Let the crucible of light which is your own heart centre build a bridge into the heart centre of the flower or plant (ask the Angel to locate this for you and she will gently guide your attention to it). Generate a wave of unconditional love and blessing from your heart to strengthen the bridge and ask to be welcomed into Fairyland. You will intuitively sense whether or not the way is open to you. If it is, proceed across the bridge, requesting that the Angel should go with you, hand in hand.

When you step into the heart centre of the flower or plant, you will begin to sense the etheric life about you, and, as you practise this meditation, you will begin to enter deeper and deeper into the realms of faery – only always ensure that you are accompanied by the Angel.

While in meditation, talk to the fairies. Tell them how much you appreciate their work in the garden. Explain that human beings are only despoilers because they are so ignorant of the truths that lie behind the kernel of life. Reassure them of your willingness to work with them. Ask them to show themselves to you as you work in the garden when they are ready to do so.

Listen, too, because the fairies will have much wisdom to impart concerning the care of the garden and the needs of the soil and the plants. They can also dispense healing and understanding of the mysteries of life.

As you work with this meditation in your garden (or indoors during inclement weather; you only need a cut flower in water or a pot plant to focus on), so you will build the bridge ever more powerfully and clearly between the mortal and the faery worlds, which will help to heal the chasm that has opened up to separate us from the vital state of brotherhood we should enjoy with the Nature spirits.

When you are ready to finish the meditation, ask the Angel to guide you back over the bridge, and seal your brow, throat, heart and solar plexus centres with the silver cross shining in a ring of light. Thank the Angel and the fairies for their co-operation, and withdraw.

So that the experience of the meditation does not fade, it is as well to record it in a journal procured for the purpose. Consultation of your meditation journal should yield the strands of a fascinating pattern of insight as the months progress.

Fairy Gifts and Blessings

There are certain hours of the day, and days of the year, upon which fairies tend to show themselves to mortal eyes. They often assume the form of coloured lights, which have been described as white, golden or many-coloured in hue, literally like the lights we hang on the Christmas tree. When they are working within the structure of plants, their vital energies can be seen by sensitives as a gossamer globe sparking with motes of light. Certainly the fairies are shape-shifters, but the form in which they most delight, and perhaps their true form, is that akin to the human being. Occultists tell us that the human form is sacred and an image of God, not in any narrow or literal sense but rather as a divinely inspired structure which is the aspirant of the creative forces, urging them to achieve union with the Godhead. Thus it is that the angels, the mighty spirits of the planets and the natural forces, the elementals and the fairies (not forgetting ourselves, of course!) all express this human configuration to some mutable degree.

So it is in beloved human form that we will begin to see the fairies; and it will help us to acquire fairy vision if we take note of the particular hours and days when the fairy people most readily appear to our circumscribed sight. The best hours are sunrise, noon, dusk, early evening and midnight; bright starlit nights and the nights of the new or full moon are especially propitious. When the moon rises in a halo, or her face shines clear golden (not the dull, brassy gold which foretells squally weather), then the night will be a fine one upon which to practise fairy vision.

When venturing outside at the fairy hours, if it is not warm enough to sit comfortably in meditation to see the fairies, simply go about ordinary gardening tasks while keeping an eye out – you might catch sight of the fairy life gathering around the boles of the trees or

floating among the flowers. Some people will find that this brings better results than a formal meditation, although it is always wise to ask the help of the Angel of the Garden and to make your attempt to develop fairy vision very clear and vivid in your mind.

FAIRY DAYS

Just as there are hours of the day when we are most likely to see the fairy folk, so there are days of the year which are particularly beneficial. The best are: New Year's Eve and New Year's Day, Twelfth Night (6 January), Imbolc (1 February), Candlemas (2 February), the first day of spring (21 March), Lady Day (25 March), Easter Day, May Eve (Walpurgis Night), May Day (Beltane), Whit Sunday, the first day of summer (21 June), Midsummer Eve (23 June), Midsummer Day (24 June), Lammas Eve (31 July), Lammastide (1 August), the first day of autumn (21 September), Hallowe'en (31 October), Samhain (11 November), the first day of winter (21 December), Christmas Eve and Christmas Day.

The days and vigils (eves) of the saints are also good days to develop fairy vision, as they are blessed with special vibrations. Information on the feast days of saints can be found in diaries, calendars and almanacs. Tuesdays, Thursdays, Fridays and Sundays are particularly fruitful days for fairy-watching, although every day of the week has its particular attributes, so none gives a poor auspice for such activity.

THE FAIRY BLESSING

Here is Sarah Greaves' advice on how to attract the Fairy Blessing to your garden:

> Be sure never to uproot or otherwise kill an established plant or tree [I think we may safety assume that transplanting is permissible]; when you remove what are known as 'weeds', do it kindly, and never when the herbs are in bloom. If you can put them to good use for food, medicine or craft-working, then the heart of Nature is appeased. If not, let

In Early Spring, John William Inchbold, 1830-88

them rot as compost, to be recycled according to Nature's plan. Everything that is uprooted must be treated with care and respect, and thanked for its appearance in your garden, however inconvenient that may seem. Each 'weed' in the garden can be used for the good of our health, or for the healing and restoration of the soil. Tend and talk to each plant and tree, give them courage to grow. Thus you will touch their spirit, and the spirit of the garden likewise. Do not listen to those who tell you that this behaviour seems a mite touched, for your garden will flourish like Paradise, whilst theirs remains commonplace.

While the tiny fairies are always at work wherever there is plant life, it is an unfortunate truth that the larger fairies have tended to desert our gardens and countryside because of our contemptuous treatment of the landscape.

As has already been described, we can do much to entice them back into our gardens so that they may bless and nurture them. Here are further instructions from the manuscripts of Sarah Greaves to encourage their return:

TO WORK A FAIRY SPELL

Pluck vervain and yarrow, mistletoe and rue, thyme and bay; dice each leaf and bake them into a little oaten cake, which must be sweetened with honey and three drops of rose-oil. Take it, freshly baked, at the time of the full moon, or at moonrise on Lady Day, Walpurgis Night, May Day, Midsummer's Eve and Midsummer's Day, Candlemas Day or Lammas-tide, Christmas Day, Christmas Eve, Hallowe'en, Easter Day or Whitsuntide, or any day or eve of the saints, and set it under a tree or a bush in a little wild spot in your garden or just beyond its boundaries. Bless the cake and say:

> Fairies, the work of my spirit I give thee,
> Be lovers true to my garden, I bid thee.

If the cake can be placed as you watch the moon rising, and if it be a

Flowering Hawthorn, Benjamin Perkins

waxing moon, that is all the better. You will know if your craft is good, for you will begin to see a new radiance steal into the blooms and a fresh vigour vivifying all the garden. Furthermore, you will perceive fairy rings where the folk of Elfame hold their revels. It may be that on still summer nights, or yet at dawn on a spring morning, you hear a fairy piping, which is the wildest, reediest sound mortal ears ever gladdened to. You will notice their woven baths in the bushes, which are like tiny, silvery hammocks spun from spiders' webs; these are sustenance for their own dancing, luminous selves. And you may note that your flowers and trees, of themselves, begin to form natural bowers and arbours, exquisite in their beauty and magical artistry, fit for the finest queen.

There is also an ancient spell for entering into the fairy joy and jubilation, rather more adventurous than the meditation previously given (although the former working is just as efficacious):

MIDSUMMER EVE FAIRY SPELL

Seek out a sequestered spot, wild and lovely, where all the herbs and trees of the summer flourish around you. Build a little fire in a ring of stones and smoulder nine pine cones and a little incense, for these do honour to the Goddess. You will have brought with you a crown twisted from oak leaves, rosemary and wild roses, pink and white. Take only what you need from each tree and bush, and bless each one for its providence.

You must wait till the twilight comes on and the stars begin to twinkle, and then dance around the fire. The fairies will show you how; listen in your heart to their inspiration, and you will dance the magical dance of the grove and the stars and the fire-bewitched night; for what was done in days of old will be done again.

When you have grown weary, sit down in a comfortable spot and dwell with deep thoughts upon the fire, which you must feed so that it springs up into life once more. Look into its flames, and ask the King of the Elves and the Queen of the Woods to be with you in your meditations. Think of the Goddess and the God, and you will feel the

When Apples were Golden and Songs were Sweet (detail),
John Melhuish Strudwick, 1849-1937

mystical forces in Nature which are the angels and the fairies. If you keep a faithful stillness of heart, soul and frame, you will see them dancing among the trees, and the fire will bring you visions of the spirit. As the fire burns down, bless your crown and lay it aside. Intone clearly, 'This is for the fairies.' Then wash yourself, in your imagination, in a great shaft of light which you must see as rays coming down from highest heaven. Put out your fire and walk home to bed. Keep a pen and paper by your bedside, for your dreams will be touched by the magic of the night and the fairies.

The dance around the fire imitates the fairy revels, although if the spell is to be worked in the garden a measure of privacy is necessary unless the neighbours are particularly enlightened!

It is worthwhile to practise the meditations and spells given, because many small miracles can be wrought in your garden when wise and loving contact with the fairies has been established. It is important to ask, and to visualize what you desire, whether it be roses blooming in the snow, out of season flowering, extended flowering seasons, altered flower colours or enriched fragrance. Verdant and abundant growth, and a delightful and singular radiance of hue of the blooms and flowers, are the first simple rewards of communing with the fairies and the Angel of the Garden.

Speak to the fairies naturally and unself-consciously, praising them for their diligence and their art. When you make a request, thank them in advance for their co-operation, and always hold them and the garden in the light of the star, asking the Angel to help you to open your heart so that the light may stream forth unimpeded. This is *your* gift to the fairies, and your fulfilment of the contract you make with them when you request them to work for you.

In our contemplations upon the Earth Angel as we sit or work in the garden, we will gradually come closer to the heart of truth. A heavy veil of materialism lies across our vision at present; yet that veil must be torn apart before we can claim the great heritage of life which is ours – the heritage of expanded consciousness.

As we envision all the forces of Nature, personified

as lesser angels, Nature gods and the fairies, dancing eternally among the cosmic robes of the Earth Angel, so we draw near to our own Angel of the Garden, because we will understand ever more clearly her source and her connection with all the other angels of the hierarchy. At the same time, she will become our personal and trusted companion, a very close and dear friend from whom to seek advice and help. This unfolding of parallel understanding by no means represents a duality, but rather allows us to perceive a balance between the individual and the whole in all creation. Once this balance between 'the dewdrop and the ocean' is truly understood, we spontaneously and naturally begin to create conditions of harmony and beauty in every aspect of our lives.

People with psychic vision can actually see threads of light connecting the simplest fairy workers with their brethren on a higher plane, the individualized fairies. These in turn are attached by this linkage of light to nobler fairy beings, who exercise a wider circumference of influence in the Nature kingdom. As the silver threads reach each higher level, they collect together into a kind of lovers' knot and rise again to the next plane where, in the order described so far, the angels themselves begin to appear, lovingly and joyfully guiding and directing the fairies.

When we view in this way the interconnectedness of all life, we can begin to understand that we are similarly joined at the soul and spiritual level with each aspect of creation; it has been given to us to embrace every dimension, however limited in mind and perception we may be at the moment. Therefore, because of the gift of this supreme opportunity, it depends on us to establish contact with the angels and the fairies. We can do this best by believing in them, appreciating them, talking to them and by developing 'enchanted vision' so that we can see them.

There are three deeply significant factors to bear in mind in developing enchanted vision:

i) that seeing the fairies, and looking deep into the heart of Nature and her exquisite secret worlds, are attributes of the *physical* eye which are stimulated by awareness and understanding in the human soul; therefore we have to work on the atrophied area of the physical organ by gradually developing and exercising our soul awareness, and it will begin to struggle out of its present state of desuetude;

ii) that meditation, contemplation and simple ceremonial acts made in faith are a sure and safe method to pursue in developing this enchanted vision of the physical eye;

iii) that *imagination*, that wise variety which is guided and controlled by the heart and which we can refer to as Creative Imagination, is the key to beginning to see clearly and truthfully; imagination is our key to the door of wonders and will unfold our enchanted vision; it must not be inhibited by prevailing mental limitations, but must be guided by seeking the jewel of truth which lies deep in the heart.

The contemplation of art, and especially the reading of poetry, assists the development of enchanted vision. Many artists and poets could and can see the fairies. Choose whatever stirs you and make a habit of reading it when resting in the garden.

Once awareness of the individualized fairies has been achieved (even if actual fairy vision does not develop, the fairy spells and meditations will undoubtedly bring a gradual recognition of the presence of fairies), it is time to move on to the apperception of a yet more sublime wonder. In communion again with the Angel of the Garden, in the magical silence to be found deep within the heart, listen to her voice as she makes all things known to her pupil, from the marvels of her angelic thought forms which are the flowers, to the Earth Mysteries which the noble beings who are trees enshrine and protect. Especially will she speak to us of the secrets of trees, and of how we can receive them into ourselves by courtesy of the ardent and exquisitely conscious tree spirits . . .

Roses, Benjamin Perkins

In a dark tree there hides
A bough, all golden, leaf and pliant stem
Sacred to Proserpine. This all the grove
Protects, and shadows cover it with darkness.
Until this bough, this bloom of light, is found,
No one receives his passport to the darkness
Whose queen requires this tribute. In succession,
After the bough is plucked, another grows,
Gold-green with the same metal. Raise the eyes,
Look up, reach up the hand.
Virgil, *Aeneid VI*

Tree Spirits

If you approach a tree with heart-centred sensitivity, palms upward and fingers splayed, you will feel the soul emanations from the tree spirit. These will almost always be friendly and benevolent; it is only in a few rare instances that they may be malevolent and hostile. This is because trees earth and imprison ill-willed and wrathful forces. The true tree spirits have nothing to do with such demonic forces; they are simply serving humanity and the planet by holding them in the fastnesses of their being, which constitutes physical strength and spiritual might.

The tree fauns, which are the male tree spirits, are kindly and wise and, though they are more reserved in their response to humankind than the female tree nymphs, are apt to fall in love with women who are sensitive to Nature, and to court their human souls, from which they long to learn. The tree nymphs behave in similar vein towards men, although they are bolder and more adventurous, and will even seek to marry their lovers by assuming human form. Many tales are told all over the world regarding this eerie phenomenon; yet the human husband invariably loses his strange and lovely wife after a time because she is still bound to her tree. No matter how far a tree faun or nymph may wander, they are linked to their tree by a palpable soul bond which psychically sensitive people can see as misty ribbons of white ether.

It would be wrong to think of the tree as merely an empty shell of matter where the tree spirit dwells. The truth is much more mysterious. The physical shape and being of the tree are mystic, and the tree and its spirit share a symbiotic relationship, each growing and learning and fusing its being with the other, until at a certain point in time, when the tree has reached maturity and is ready to express grandeur, it raises its vibrations, lifts itself somewhat beyond the group soul of its species and begins to individuate. The tree spirit retreats further and deeper *within* the physical and astral dimensions of the tree rather than wandering about outside the tree as an external soul; it begins to understand and to dwell in the psycho-spiritual world of which its tree is such a profound member. Then the tree wakens from its ancient dreaming consciousness and becomes an individual, a person.

These mighty, time-honoured, wise and sentient beings give to the landscape where they stand a beautiful and awe-inspiring feeling of solemnity. Their soul reaches to the highest Heavens and their roots penetrate the deepest secrets of the sacred Earth. They become rooted and embodied angels, in communion with the purely spiritual angels who guard the solitude of the forests and the sanctified places which must not be despoiled.

The great, ancient, ensouled trees watch over us and mediate between Heaven and Earth, God and humanity. These are the sacred trees under whom the Buddha received his enlightenment. Many saints, mystics and poets, musicians and Wise Brethren, both men and women, received their knowledge and teachings from the mighty spirits of evolved trees.

Above all, it is good to remember how truly united are the hearts and souls of trees and of humanity. We should aim to look steadily through the obscuring mists of materiality which would steal our spiritual birthright from us, and see the blessed opportunities which are ours to respond with love and humility to the noble tree beings which beautify our surroundings and make them holy. Trees need to receive our love as they need to give us their own, which they do constantly, with a free hand and heart. We would not be able to survive on this Earth plane were it not for the trees. Even little saplings can be nurtured by our love, so that they soon become beings of wisdom and spiritual might. When the great and ancient trees co-operate with us in spiritual magic motivated by love for humanity and all creation, the results of such spiritual outpourings are increased a thousandfold.

If you are lucky enough to have a tree of great age growing in your garden, you would do well to initiate a loving relationship with it, and, when the weather is mild, to sleep out under its sheltering branches, if only for an hour or two. The tree will give you comfort, strength and wise counsel, which you will soon be able to receive directly, in the conscious state.

Because of their noble and magical qualities of spirit and soul, tree-tops bear secrets within them which are truly astounding. They act as perfect astral platforms for higher beings to sit and look out at us.

Angels and spirit guides, beings from etherealized planets which are invisible to us (both their planets and themselves), gods and saints and other highly evolved souls can all seat themselves in tree-tops and commune with us. When seeking for guidance or inspiration for any project in life, we can go to the trees and rely both on them and on the beings they host for kindly response, which will embrace not only our own individual good, but the good of the community at large and beyond to all creation, for each tiny act we perform, each thought and each word resonate in the cosmos.

The trees and the spiritual beings accompanying them know the secret of the balance between the individual and the whole, the one and the many. It is a matter of becoming accustomed to greeting and receiving guidance and enlightment from these beings in the tree-tops. They would teach us that the kindly trees are guardians of our human souls, and ever seek to uplift our spirit and our vision. We receive from the trees and from the beings in the tree-tops in equal measure. In this way, as we begin to expand our consciousness, the garden can truly become a place of sanctified communion.

TREES OF MERCY

Lovers have anciently composed a language of flowers and claimed it as their own; yet garden trees and flowers, and their companions from the wild which stray in and wantonly take root, speak a wiser and a stranger language. This magical language springs from the heart of our folklore, that crucible of human imagination and mythopoetic perception, of planetary dimensions and familiar and eternal cycles in every language and culture, which still smoulders subliminally in us today, and which can illumine our vision and fire our understanding of those mysterious aspects of life for which Nature provides so many profound and lovely symbols.

Each tree which takes root in the garden, or is purposefully planted there, speaks of a symbol beyond its immediate physical reality, and conveys to sensitive percipience an ever-present message. All are healers, yet some bear merciful properties and virtues which are specific to the human condition.

Titian's First Essay in Colour (detail), William Dyce, 1806-64

THE APPLE TREE, CUSTODIAN OF WISDOM

The apple tree is a magical tree of the Goddess. In the northern myth cycles, Freya, goddess of wisdom and fecundity, trod the paths of Heaven, dispensing golden apples to the gods so that they might partake of her cherished gifts of calm, reflective wisdom and understanding.

For the sake of the knowledge of the sacred apple, Eve cast away the delights and sanctuary of Eden, and, Prometheus-like, risked the anger of God, even though the mysterious transubstantiation-in-reverse which came about through her mystical act of eating the apple brought her sorrow, loss, the bitterness of earthly experience, old age and death. Such are the initiations of the Underworld through which she, in her wisdom as Mother of Men, chose to journey. The world of matter, which is the Goddess-world, is represented by the apple. If the fruit is cut in two, one sees clearly in the sliced core the image of female genitalia, the magical gates of rebirth. Yet the apple tree is a tree of healing, and to eat daily of its fruit has long been recognized as a panacea to keep all ills at bay.

When planting a group of apple trees in the garden, bear in mind that as age begins to breathe its hoar upon them, they will assume gnarled and twisted postures fantastic in shape and suggestion. This is because they are expressing their role as aged priestesses of the garden. Let them flourish, then, close to the other plants and trees of the plot, rather than isolating them in an orchard. If you have planned an orchard, plant it so that the trees overlook the rest of the garden. By so doing, you will ensure that the spirit of the garden grows and endures in wisdom.

The apple tree is indeed a tree of happy omen to grow in the garden, for the Druids said it grew in the Celtic paradise and was the custodian of all knowledge. Their lore teaches that the day of the apple tree is Friday (Freya's day) and its star is Venus, goddess of the rose. The rose and the apple tree are of the same family, and lay claim to the same spiritual birthright, which is to symbolize in their essence the secret heart of humanity, and to proffer the qualities and virtues which heal and nurture the seed of the spirit that lies hidden within. When King Arthur was taken beyond the veil into the Otherworld,

Garden Crab Apples, Benjamin Perkins

for the healing of his wounds, the place to which he was carried was called the Vale of Avalon – the Apple Vale. Those who are familiar with Arthurian symbolism will recognize the teaching here, in that Arthur is the emblem of humanity's higher self, which ever strives towards the attainment of knowledge of the Godhead, and yet is wounded by the fell blows and hideous poison of the mortal world. The apple tree, sign of the soul and the harbourer of Goddess-wisdom, is the one true antidote.

Watch to see if the sun shines through the apple trees on Christmas morning, and on Easter morning too, for that foretells a plentiful, healthy crop and a year of smiling prosperity for the keeper of the garden or the apple orchard. If the fruit is blessed by rain on St Peter's Day (29 June) or St Swithin's Day (15 July) it will impart serene spirits and the bloom of health to all who eat of it.

In September, summertide's rich golden evening, do not strip the tree bare, for that is unlucky and offends the Goddess, whose ever-yielding graces deplore greed and robbery. Leave one or two of her sacred fruits to hang on the tree for the birds, and you will fare all the better. Wisewomen will tell you that these remaining apples are not for the birds alone, but to honour the fairies and the ancient spirit of the orchard, which dwells in every apple tree.

If there are a number of trees, be sure that in the most ancient of them all dwells the Apple Tree Man, the guardian of their fertility and the fairy protector of the spirit of the Goddess. It is for the sake of this Apple Tree Man that the custom of wassailing the apple trees is performed upon old Twelfth Night (17 January). For this, you must repair to the orchard, or to the apple tree in the garden, choose the eldest and drink to it by taking a sip from a tankard of cider which you have mulled over ashen-wood. Throw the rest over its gnarled roots, and place a mite of toast which has been steeped in cider in a fork of its boughs. All of your company must bow three times to the tree and dance around it in a spirit of great merriment. If you have a drum on which you can beat out a sprightly rhythm, so much the better. Pipes, whistles and clapping will please the Apple Tree Man. This ceremony is called apple wassailing, sometimes known as apple howling. Here is the old song which must be sung to the Apple Tree Man:

The Beguiling of Merlin (detail), Sir Edward Burne-Jones, 1833-95

Hail to thee, Old Apple Tree!
And Hail to thee, Lady!
Stand fast, root,
Bear well, top!
Pray God send us a good howling crop!
Every twig, apples big!
Every bough, apples enow!
Hats full, caps full,
Full quarter sack full!
Ho! The Apple Blessing on all our homes and crops,
On heart and hearth, on bairns and flocks!
Holla, lasses! Holla, lads!
Huzzah!

Drink to the health of one another, and to that of the community at large; then bid goodnight to the Apple Tree Man and to the Lady, and return to your homes, where you must stay, fast indoors, whatever strange sounds you may hear without, for the deepest magic is abroad, and it is not right that mortal eyes should observe it.

In this way, the happiest blessing is procured for the year ahead. In the spring, grow an abundance of foxgloves next to the apple trees, for the foxglove is a fairy flower and pleases the Goddess and the Apple Tree Man. Let lupins grow plentifully among your apple trees as well, for they are sure to improve the quality of the fruit. Nasturtiums will protect the trees from woolly aphids and whitefly if you allow their cunning tendrils to twine around their trunks, for these flowers, all the trinity, protect and honour the Goddess. If you heed this advice, you will find that your apple crop stores longer and tastes sweeter.

APPLE SPELLS

To cure a wart, divide an apple in two, rub the excrescence with both halves, tie them together again and bury the whole in the earth. The wart will disappear as the incarcerated fruit moulders away.

If you have an ailing plant or tree which will not respond to plant medicine, take an apple, perfect in roundness and health, bless it by holding it in the rays of the heart and carving a little cross into its flesh, saying:

The Apple Blessing encompass you, sickly one;
Magic sphere so round and firm
Take away the blighting worm
Breathe your spirit o'er this that fails
Breathe until the demon quails,
Strength and beauty restore to thee
Vigour of blossom and fruit shall be
The Apple Blessing encompass you, sickly one,
The Apple Blessing encompass you.

Then bury it close to the fading plant. Ask the fairies to help you in your healing endeavours, and renew the power of the rune by chanting it at noon each day over the buried apple until all is well.

For a red or coarse complexion, gather May dew and steep apple blossom in it, heating all over a fire of ashen-wood. Bless this apple-blossom water and apply it to the skin, leaving it to dry of itself. Ask a blessing of beauty and purity from the Goddess, and the magic of her divine tree will heal your complaint.

THE BLESSED ROWAN

The delicate-leaved rowan with its clusters of autumn berries that delight the eye is called by countryfolk the 'witch' or 'wicken tree', and so is revealed as a tree sacred to the Goddess. If its seed roots naturally in the garden, then that garden is blessed indeed and enjoys the favour and protection of the fairies.

The rowan or mountain ash is a Druid tree, one of the holy trees of this ancient Celtic brotherhood of the forests; its wood, foliage and bonny scarlet berries were revered ingredients in their magical arts. The rowan turns away all evil and thrives upon sites where once stood Druidic stone circles, or land where Druidic rites and perambulation have blessed the soil. When the rowan is hung with a rich crop of burgeoning berries, it is said that the earthly remains of some sainted soul lie buried nearby. Even if, say the old wise-saws, a sprinkling of their antique dust is all that quietly remains in the earth, the essence of their goodness and wisdom endures, and is celebrated and tenderly protected by the ardent branches of the wicken tree.

The fairies often adopt a lone wicken tree as their own, making a palace within its etheric body and below its roots deep and far into the earth. The rowan is one of that special trilogy – oak, ash and thorn – which protects from malignant spirits and all forms of psychic attack. The rowan tree is a holy tree and a fairy tree, for there is no division between sanctity and the fairies, although orthodoxy has traditionally claimed that there is.

If your garden is without a rowan, plant one in a tranquil spot and give the young tree your heartfelt care. Then your souls will unite one with the other, and if danger or illness should threaten you or yours, the rowan will speak a warning of it by falling listless and withering a little in its growth. When it flourishes fine and strong, fortune is sure to smile upon you; and in all the calamities of your life, the wicken tree will be to you a source of protection and comfort, and shelter for your soul. Water the young tree well each and every day for a year and a day after planting, and bless the water each Monday and Friday of the week by holding your hands aloft over the pail and whispering a prayer to the Goddess to send a stream of light from your heart down into the water. This you will breathe forth from the exalted organ as if you were weaving a skein of silver stars into the depths of that mysterious reflective element.

Above all, remember that the wicken tree is proud. It will not gladly suffer other plants to touch it or to grow too near; therefore be counselled to leave a little space clear around its bole, for honour's sake. The secret of the majesty of this spiritual tree and its regal Goddess powers is celebrated on 3 May, which is Rowan Tree Day, more generally known as Holy Rood Day, the feast of the Invention of the Holy Cross. On this day, the home and all its outlying buildings should be decorated with sprigs of the rowan, to court the blessing, felicity and protection of the Goddess.

ROWAN TREE SPELLS

Upon the morning of Rowan Tree Day, venture out into the soft, dewy stillness which lies on the breast of the land in the hour before sunrise, bearing a knife with a handle of gold or silver, or brass at a pinch, which you will have sharpened and polished with care under the rays of the last full moon. Seek out a rowan tree; the first you come to will be the one to work the magic. Bow most respectfully

Ripe Rowan Berries, Benjamin Perkins

to the spirit of the tree and chant this rune:

> Witch tree, rowan tree, pretty mountain ash,
> Protect me right well from storm, flood and flash;
> Now do I beg of thee some wee twigs and leaves,
> And pri'thee turn from me all harm and griefs.

Take your knife, and tenderly cut away a palmful of foliage, making sure you do no damage. Now you must say:

> I thank thee, wicken tree,
> I thank thee, Lady!

and after bowing three times, you may turn your steps homeward, only be very certain to traverse a different route to that you came by. The rowan leaves will give you a pocketful of goodly charms, which may be slipped into your purse and your shoe, your handkerchief and your apron, to bring you good luck and favour, and safety to your person; and if you hang a little sprig over the hearth and over your bed, the beneficent charm will also be worked. If you keep animals, put a little over the stable door or near the byre, and the spell will work likewise. A twelvemonth will the charm hold good; then the magic must be worked again.

Wear a sprig of rowan in your hair when you ride upon your horse, and the Goddess spirit in it will speak to your steed, and calm and soothe the beast, so that you come to no harm and your journey will be swift and untroubled, in whatever wise it may please you to travel, for the Goddess weaves a journeyer's charm about those travellers who wear her sign and signature in their hair.

Thread a necklace of scarlet berries from the rowan tree, and if you walk consciously in the Goddess's presence when wearing it, she will give you beauty of form and face and smile most benignantly upon you so that you walk always in a charmed circle. The wood of the rowan, too, brings down the blessings of the Goddess. It is lucky for children and animals, and all tender, newborn things, which the Goddess folds unto her heart.

Make a rowan garland in the joyful rays of the sun, and place it around the waist of an expectant mother near her time, so that the pangs of birth will be eased for her when the good hour comes.

Make a rowan garland in the enchanted hush of the beams of the moon, and give it to one who suffers from the racks of rheumatism. Then will his pains be soothed all away, so that however scornful he may heretofore have been in making great game of it, he will henceforth respect most profoundly the art of wortcunning – that is, the knowledge of the properties of herbs and how to apply them for healing and magic – and its practitioners, all his life long.

HAZEL, TREE OF THE STAR GODDESS

The hazel tree is associated with the Celtic goddess of the stars, Arianrhad, the Mother Goddess whose image and grand courts the early Celts saw in what we know today as the constellation of the Corona Borealis and the sky-spanning bridge of the Milky Way. This majestic Mother Goddess of the stars blessed the hazel, one of the traditional holy trees of the Druids, with virtues and powers which were the guardians of wisdom and knowledge, poetry and fire, beauty and fecundity.

Perhaps because of this association, hazel was one of the nine sacred woods used in making the Need-fire on May Day (the Celtic festival of Beltane). Need-fire was the new fire, created from friction carried out in sunwise (clockwise) rotation and brought to each household for rekindling in the hearth after the old fire had been extinguished. The bearers of the fire were young men, 'pure in word and deed', who travelled from east to west to follow the path of the sun. These young men also created the fire by the prescribed method of friction, and leapt over the bonfire as it began to die down, driving their oxen before them through the purifying flames.

As the hazel is the tree of divine fire, so it is also the tree of benign witchcraft and magic. It is sometimes called the 'tree of wishes' because it has power to grant the heart's desire, as long as the wish is wise and reflects a true need.

Grow a little grove of hazel trees, if you can, so that the space among them may be a shrine to its powers and virtues. The trees need be only three in number, if your garden is small. Watch the moon rise through their branches, and the gentle stars of the evening too as they scintillate the first dusk with silver, because these celestial firefolk will bring you intimations of the secrets of the hazel tree, and draw you close to its magical heart.

Hesperus, Sir Joseph Noel Paton, 1821-1901

HAZEL SPELLS

Gather a little bundle of hazel twigs on Palm Sunday, bless them in the name of the Goddess, tie them with white ribbon and hang them near the hearth. You will thus have a charm that turns away lightning and calamities from the home.

As fire is the physical form of the sacred essence of the Godhead, so in days of old a divine flame was kept alight upon ancient altars. When we think of the Star Goddess and her emblem of flame, so we may perceive that her tree, the hazel, blessed as a spiritual symbol of holy fire, will heal and protect our own altar, the human heart. If a palmful of hazel nuts is eaten each day in ponderance and consciousness of this holiness of the human organ and the flame of pure spiritual light which burns therein, they will be sure to improve and protect the heart, and the life of the wise one who follows this counsel will ripen into a grand old age.

Eat daily of the nuts of the hazel to nourish the poet, the scholar and the lover within you.

Take of the milk of the hazel nut as a charm for health and fortune, and give it to bairns in the cradle, for their blessing. Weave hazel sprigs into a chaplet and wear it in your hair; if you do this on May Day you will have good luck all year, and will have three wishes granted to you besides.

Tell the weather by observing the season's crop of hazel nuts. If their shells are thin, expect a gentle winter, soon gone; but if their shells are thick, the winter is likely to be hoary and blighting, full of storms and drifts of snow, chasing the skirts of spring well into the middle of April.

THE FRAGRANT BAY, TREE OF HEALING

The handsome bay tree is associated with the masculine principle and the old gods. It is a tree of the Lord, and its spiritual virtues are connected with medicine, music and the rays of the sun. The bay protects dwellings, gardens and those who inhabit them from disease and the Evil Eye. Its fragrance is rumoured to revive even those whose spirit has left the Earth in death; it calls them back to their physical vehicle with its music and healing. It is a symbol of the Christ when he said, 'I am the Life and the Resurrection.'

The essence of the bay celebrates valour, honour and human triumph. Its leaves crowned heroes, poets and victors, and where the bay withered, the death of kings or men of high renown was foretold.

Grow the bay tree in a pot near the house door, for the tree wards off thunder and illness, of the heart and soul as well as of the material body and the elements. Its aroma, which is both sharp and sweet, drives away ill-omened spirits and favours well-disposed fairies.

BAY SPELLS

Pin bay leaves to your pillow so that you may dream charmed healing dreams, and especially try this upon St Valentine's Eve, for they will bring to you the shade of your future marriage partner, whom you will see in your sleep.

Burn one or two bay leaves on your fire at fall of dusk, and put a question to the spirit of the tree and to the salamanders who dance in the flames. If they crackle and spit vigorously in their burning, the portent is good. If they are consumed in silence, the omen bids you accept disappointment with a stalwart heart.

If the bay falters in its growth, it foretells a time of trial which will be felt by all the nation; sometimes a bay tree will wither in mourning when a member of the household passes beyond the veil.

The spirit of the bay is valiant and it cannot tolerate the clinging vine. Therefore, take care not to plant your bay tree where vines grow nearby, for neither will flourish in the other's company.

When a babe is first born, it is lucky to celebrate the happy event by planting a bay tree in the little one's honour. If there is a bay already growing in your garden, cuttings for this purpose, taken in April, will fare best.

THE OAK, LORD OF TRUTH

The oak is a sacred tree. Its spirit is ancient and wise, and it is said that the rustling of its leaves is the whispering voice of Jupiter. There is in its very being a knowledge of the elixir of life, the Secret Flame Within, which is the origin and the essence of Earth's humanity – its vitality and its source. Its mighty spirit blesses and protects, its kindly heart gives peace, its noble boughs give shelter. Wisewomen tell of the Oakman who laments whenever one of these kingly trees is felled.

Such an act is doubly dangerous, because it is abhorrent to the great Nature gods, who can become destructive when their wrath is roused, and because the oak can lock spiteful demons within the majestic might of its body, quelling their dark energies and rendering their malice harmless.

The oak is a thunder tree and will give protection from the flash when its spirit is called upon, even when it has itself been struck by lightning. The Druids worshipped the oak, and the precious mistletoe to which it is host.

OAK SPELLS

Put a handful of oak leaves in your bath, and you will be cleansed both in body and in spirit. An oak leaf worn at your breast, touching your heart, will preserve you from deception and the world's false glamour. Remember that the tree is Lord of Truth. Meditate under its mighty branches, and you will see into your heart with unsullied vision, what is good there and also that which needs to be swept away or transformed.

He or she that would dream true, let them embrace the oak three times before going to bed, and put that question which their soul longs to have answered to the spirit of the tree. If it is right for them to have such knowledge, the Oakman will step into their sleeping visions and by his cunning arts vouchsafe to them a prophetic dream.

The oak is the tree of marriage between the God and the Goddess. It is the tree of Robin Hood and Maid Marian, who are their earthly representatives. If, on your wedding day, you dance three times sunwise around an oak tree soon after the marriage ceremony, and wear one of its leaves in your buttonhole or bouquet, long years and happy tears will bless the conjugal knot. Carve a little cross upon a bough of your chosen oak, and let the bride leave the Oakman a flower and the groom a lock of his hair.

YOUR OWN HEALING TREE

When you have ascertained that a tree has kindly and loving emanations (see page 40), you can actually transfer your own pain and suffering (mental or physical) to it should you become ill. Sit at its bole and embrace the tree with both arms, and ask the spirit of the tree to take your burden from you. Do this each day until you feel relief. Each time after you make the request, bless and thank the tree for its act of healing.

You may like to select such a tree with which to create a life bond. Your souls will be united, and the tree will give you its strength, its wisdom, and a certain invincible quality. Be certain never to abuse any of these gifts, and your tree will be a true friend, helping you to steer your course through life while succouring your soul with its great gripping roots so that you will never lose your mental or physical moorings. Even when a person is far away from their tree, its healing properties, strength, comfort, wisdom and sanctuary can still be called upon. Your soul will visit the tree in your dreams, and the bond between you will be nourished and reinforced.

THE TREE DANCE

To dance the Tree Dance for absorbing energy and giving it out again to the garden is an exercise that benefits and pleases the trees, the tree spirits and the fairies. The Tree Dance is closely related to the fairy dances or revels, in which they create a shining etheric ball of subtle energized substance (like a battery) which is discharged into the flowers and trees and grasses of the area they care for. The Tree Dance can be done with or without musical accompaniment. Folk music or harp music is best.

Perform the Tree Dance by imitating the whirling dervishes of the Sufis, simply skipping in and out among the tree boles, or by performing the grander, more stately perambulation in which one proceeds by taking three steps forward and one step back, walking in rhythm among the trees. Or you can perform a dance of your own devising that you create from inspiration and guidance emanating directly from the trees. Asking consciously to be given the form of the Tree Dance helps your spirit to be suffused and permeated by the enlightenment of tree wisdom, so that the inspiration of the dance will quicken first your soul and then your feet.

While performing the Tree Dance, it is important consciously to gather the energies of the spiritual and etheric forces playing around you into yourself as a focal point, and then, when you feel you are a whirling, skipping or striding column of golden energy, give forth this gathered, concentrated force into the heart of the garden. Afterwards

The Bower Meadow, Dante Gabriel Rossetti, 1828-82

you will feel energized because the human heart is a source of ever-renewing spiritual power and cannot be exhausted. Sometimes you may feel that the fairies and the tree spirits, or even the god of Nature, Pan himself, dance with you. This is a blessing, and shows that you are performing the Tree Dance rite with true attunement. If the Goddess dances with you, you will take back into your human life the fruits of art and beauty, magic and enchantment, and a fund of the Goddess wisdom.

The importance of dancing and the expression of joy in the creation of the enchanted garden cannot be overestimated – not dancing which is an expression of human ego and sexuality, nor dancing which reinforces social inhibitions, but rather dancing which is a simple and natural expression of heartfelt joy.

Every area of landscape has its Lord and Lady trees. These two are the guardian trees of their little kingdom, greatest in age and wisdom among the neighbouring trees and specially blessed by the God and Goddess to be their representatives on Earth. Their influence usually extends over half a square mile. They know the past and the future and by means of this knowledge are able to channel harmony and balance into the present, the Eternal Now.

If these Lord and Lady trees reside in your garden, you are fortunate indeed and should seek to attune yourself to them. Use your outstretched hands to feel the emanations of your local trees. The psychic current from the Lord and Lady trees is very strong, warm and pulsating, and you will soon be able to distinguish it. If you do not receive such impressions, ask the Angel of the Garden to help you find the two guardian trees and set off on a spiritual nature walk. You will not have to travel very far, because the Lord and Lady trees will emit their vibrations so forcibly that you will soon begin to receive them on your open hands.

Some people can hear trees singing, and if by sensitive attunement you begin to discern the choiring of the trees, listen for a deep, dominant song from the Tree Lord, and a sweet, soft, spiritual note of feminine power from the Tree Lady.

As soon as you begin to receive the frequencies of the Lord and Lady trees, move towards them and find them, or, if this is really impossible, ask their spirits to implant an image of themselves upon your inner eye. Thus you will be able to begin to know and love these trees. They will impart the wisdom of their group and themselves to you, and you will begin to live life with a new perception of its majesty and its miraculous possibilities, and to be blessed with feelings of aspiration and high endeavour.

A marvellous way of sourcing the wisdom and forces of the Lord and Lady trees for the blessing of your garden (should these guardian trees be growing outside its boundaries) is to select a pair of trees, one masculine, one feminine, to be the recipients of the energy of the guardian trees. These may be planted together, using trees as mature as possible, if there are no trees in the garden. Good pairings include the oak and the silver birch, the ash and the hawthorn, the willow and the pine, the rowan and the holly, the hazel and the elm, the apple and the pear. Bless your selected pair with the white light, and ask the Angel of the Garden to help you in your enterprise.

Begin to meditate regularly on the images of the Lord and Lady trees, asking them to draw close to you and to enfold you in their greater cosmic being. When you feel a true telepathic communion with the guardian trees, make your request that they should channel their wise energies into the two garden trees of your choice, so that your garden may become a focal point of harmony and healing. Then, every Sunday and Monday evening for the span of several weeks, concentrate on the mystical heart centre of your two chosen trees, and see them opening up like a white rose unfolding, becoming white-light chalices ready to be filled with the secret forces from the energy fields of the Lord and Lady trees. See these spiritual emanations pouring into the heart chalices of the garden tree, and the garden trees growing in learning and soul stature as this happens.

When the process is complete, thank the Lord and Lady trees for their bounty and bless and seal with a silver cross the receptive garden trees. Make a little ceremony of this ritual, burning white candles and incense, if you can. Performed faithfully, this magical working should, over the period of a month, so fill and quicken the garden trees with subtle higher energies that they will become Lord and Lady trees of the garden in their own right. They will not vibrate upon the same elevated plane as the guardian trees, of course; but they will be wise enough to harmonize any negative energy that may exist in your garden plot, and they will bestow an atmosphere of healing, beauty, peace, enchantment and sanctuary to the garden.

Fairy Trees

Every tree has a soul (its slowly awakening consciousness) and a spirit (the supernatural being which is attached to its tree but which can move about outside it as well as withdrawing into the tree and blending with its soul) and is beloved by the fairy folk; but there are certain trees which are under the protection of the fairies. Not every specimen of its kind among the fairy trees is so honoured, certainly; but if you would grow and tend a fairy tree in your garden, it is important to know something of the history and the nature of the fairies' preference. The greatest of the fairy trees are: rowan, bramble, ash, oak, whitethorn or hawthorn (the May tree), blackthorn, elder, birch, apple, hazel, aspen, bay, lilac, osier, alder, holly, broom, pine and Scots fir.

BRAMBLE

The fairies love this wild, richly fruit-yielding bush. Its branches protect the sanctity of the wilderness, catching fast hold of hair and clothes so that intrusive humans cannot penetrate the fairy clearings and secret wooded places. The Nature spirits love to receive a gift of homemade bramble jelly, put into a little pot marked 'for the good folk' and buried near to the bramble bush.

ASH

The stories surrounding the ash are manifold. It is said to be an ancestor of humankind, and in Greece certain powerful families were believed to be descended from ash trees. Jove created the third, brazen race of men from them, and when the Norse gods desired to populate their freshly created sublunary world with a newborn race, they breathed a human soul into the body and spirit of an ash tree; the first man came forth and was conjoined with his mate, the first

Wild Roses, Benjamin Perkins

woman, who was created from another fairy tree, the alder; so the human race was born, blessed with an ancestry of trees. The sacred ash, Yggdrasil, was the divine structure supporting the entire universe in northern myth-cycles, and the Tree of Life meditation – which leads us to ponder on the great roots of the Holy Tree as they penetrate the heart of the Earth, the bough of the Tree as it rises heavenwards, the marvellous foliage of the Tree as it gives shelter and estate to birds, animals, mythic beasts and the upward-climbing soul paths of humankind, and the glorious tree-top as it shines with the brilliant effulgence of the radiant Godhead – is most efficaciously performed beneath the blessed boughs of the ash.

The fairies cleave to the ash because of the deeply magical energies it conducts into the Earth; and if tokens of human hair are hung upon the branches of the ash, with a request for healing of the owner of the hair, then the fairies will grant it, provided the supplicant makes the request in good faith.

LILAC

The sweet-scented lilac is one of the loveliest trees in springtime, and its potent fragrance is said to be magical, transporting mortal souls to fairyland and the supernal worlds. The amethyst and pink blooms reflect the hue of the tree sylph, while white lilac is a symbol of the liberated spirit. Perhaps because of this, an English tradition associates it with death and declares it an unlucky flower to be brought into the house. These old country customs sometimes reflect fear of the fairies, but in spite of them the lilac is a beneficent tree. Its flowers can be eaten as a tonic and are especially good for a depleted nervous system. A five-petalled lilac blossom is a bringer of luck, and the finder may request a wish from the Good Folk.

PINE

The pine is the tree of the sun. It represents the life force, rooted in Earth and aspiring heavenwards. Its triangular shape is a signature for the trinity of the Great Spirit or God, and its role as the Christmas tree links it with the glorious Sun spirit which occidental religions call

Autumn Leaves, Sir John Everett Millais, 1829-96

Christ ('the True Light'). The fairy at the top of the Christmas tree is a symbol (among others) of our human kinship with the fairy and angelic kingdoms which is fostered by the power of trees.

Meditate upon these things each Christmas-tide, and bless the tree as you carry it into the home, and also as you decorate it. It will radiate gifts of peace and hope, and its fairy life will gladden the Christmas season with joy and good cheer.

BROOM

The broomstick is famous in legend as an accoutrement of witches, giving them the power of flight and protection from their enemies. The magical influences of the broom are certainly associated with soul or astral travel, and its brilliant golden flowers delight the fairies, who will often make the secret bower of a mature broom a favourite gathering-place.

Those who prepare a cologne from the flowers in the springtime and ask the blessing of the fairies on it will procure for themselves a perfume which inspires affection, friendship and goodwill wherever they wander. To prepare a tonic for the blood, gather the tops of the young branches and make an infusion using six teaspoonsful of the herb to three-quarters of a pint of water.

ASPEN

Tradition says that the aspen tree shivers with everlasting horror because its wood was used to make the cross on Calvary. This legend is important to the magical imagination, because it links the aspen with the great cross of matter which is symbolized by the World Tree, the mystical ash tree which supports the entire physical universe.

An old spell for healing instructs the patient to make a small hole in the trunk of the aspen, fill it with nail-parings over which a blessing has been spoken and then close the hole carefully with moss or bark chippings. As the wound in the trunk heals over, the patient will similarly be made whole.

SILVER BIRCH

The lovely silver birch is a symbol of summer ever returning and is associated with Lammas-tide, the Festival of the First Fruits on the first day of August. Throughout all the festivals of the summer, it is lucky to wear a little cross fashioned from sprigs of birch. The birch is said to be one of the royal trees flowering everlastingly in Paradise, regal mother to the majestic oak, for it was the silver birch which fertilized and prepared the forest floor in prehistoric times so that the oak could begin to flourish.

This tree is associated with the light of the stars and the moon, and with our own sun at its zenith. The fairies love to make their revels in and beneath its branches during the fair spring nights, and so at this season of the year crosses made of birchwood twigs which are placed in the seed-beds will bring particular enrichment to the soil and the seedlings. May morning is especially propitious for this enterprise.

ALDER

The catkin-bearing alder resists decay in its watery habitat, so providing us with a clue concerning the secret qualities of its soul. The undines and water spirits love and protect this tree, as do the mysterious white fairy horses, linked to the unicorn, which inhabit lakes, rivers and deep pools. Water is a symbol of the human soul, and indeed of the soul life of all created things. These strange white horses, of which there are numerous reported sightings throughout the history of folklore, are covetous of the human soul, because the fairies have much to learn from it.

Alder leaves are good for kidney disorders and general dropsical conditions (add one chopped teaspoonful of the herb to a cup of boiling water, infuse for one minute and take three times daily) and this same herbal tea will also restore tired, sore feet when applied as a cooling, soothing lotion. An ancient spell is to place an alder leaf in each shoe when walking; then the fairies will bless your journey.

HOLLY

The holly tree is a symbol of the life force, and represents undiminishing vitality and the immortality of creation. It is a lucky tree to grow in the garden, because its handsome presence wards off negative and sinister influences. It is a favoured Christmas decoration because its shining evergreen leaves and its glossy red berries signify life eternal and the fire of the spirit, and so are in themselves a celebration of the returning of the light at the winter solstice.

It is lucky to burn thoroughly dried holly branches (the omen is ill if they are burned while still green); and the fairies cast their influence over the male holly tree (prickly) so that it is fortunate for men, and over the female holly (smooth and variegated) so that it is lucky for women. The Holly Man and the Holly Woman are said to inhabit their respective trees, and are protected by the fairies.

JUNIPER

In ancient times the juniper was universally loved as a protective and kindly tree, and to fell it was considered extremely unlucky. During the Flight into Egypt, Herod's soldiers were gaining fast upon the Holy Family. In desperation, the Virgin turned to a copse of trees nearby and asked them to hide her baby. At once, the juniper opened its branches to receive the Christ child, and threw a fairy glamour over Mary and Joseph so that when the soldiers overtook them they saw nothing but an old man and his elderly wife hobbling by, and passed on without enquiry.

The Book of Kings in the Bible tells us that when Elijah fled from the malice of the vengeful Queen Jezebel, he sheltered in hiding beneath the branches of a juniper tree, and there its angel visited and fed him, offering solace and hope.

Smoke from burning juniper wood wards off demons and sickness, and so strong is the fairy life within this tree that it enshrines an abundance of healing properties. Infusions (one chopped teaspoonful to one cup of boiling water) have been known to cure rheumatism and fits, kidney and liver troubles, arthritis and dropsy, and to rejuvenate the aged. A sprig of juniper, carried about the person, gives protection from ill-willed fairies and courts the blessings of the good Nature spirits.

HAWTHORN (WHITETHORN OR THE MAY TREE)

Of all the fairy trees, the hawthorn or the May tree is the wildest, the most uncompromising, the most fragrant and the most sacred to the

Early Lovers, Frederick Smallfield, 1829-1915

fairies. In our gardens and parks, while the oak emanates majesty, the birch her fair graces and other trees their various beauties and aspects of elegance, the thorn tree never adapts itself to human culture and human proximity. Its heart and spirit are unreservedly wild, and even in a town garden its form and its fragrance reach out to connect with the soul harmonic we call 'the wilderness', that beautiful place of trial and testing where the spirit of Nature holds untrammelled sway, and where every individual human soul must journey, humbled and alone, to learn enlightenment.

The Crown of Thorns is said to have been wrought from the hawthorn, representing the majesty and supreme enlightenment presented to Christ by his sojourn in the wilderness. It is a magical and a sacred tree. Sit beneath it on Walpurgis Night (May Day Eve), Lady Day, Midsummer Eve and Hallowe'en to see the fairies. Make a may garland from the hawthorn for luck, but offer a prayer first, and thank the fairies afterwards.

Make the hawthorn globe, which is a charm-ball, of its sticks and foliage. It must be made at first light on New Year's Day from last year's may foliage, and it must be tied with white ribbon. Burn the old charm-ball (i.e. one made the previous year) first on a bonfire of straw, ash twigs and acorns. That is your old self with all its troubles and sorrows being consumed; your new self forged afresh for fortune and fate is signified by the new hawthorn globe you have made, which can be kept until the next New Year.

Although the hawthorn flourished before Christ's birth, Joseph of Arimathea is said to have brought a mysterious winter-flowering whitethorn into being by striking his staff (which is a magician's tool) into the ground on Wearyall Hill when he came to Glastonbury. It thrust miraculous roots into the soil and blossomed at midnight upon Christmas Eve, flowering again in Maytime. Its daughter trees, sprung from cuttings, still bloom at Christmas-tide. Its flowering sprigs are cut and presented to the Queen each year so that they may adorn her Christmas breakfast table.

ELDER

This most powerful fairy tree has been held in awe and even deeply feared throughout the ages. Folk belief held that it was unlucky to bring elderwood or elder flowers into the house, and particularly ill-omened to burn it. This was considered to bring the devil into the home, and would cause a death in the family within the year. Farmers would not drive their cattle to market with elder sticks, nor would their wives use the wood for skewering dressed poultry. 'Ellan-wood' was never used for making cradles, or even for repairing the rockers, because this would give witches power to rock the child violently in its bed until it was injured, and otherwise bewitch it.

Stories of the feared witch or mother associated with the tree are counterbalanced by a host of stories which claim that the tree protects against witchcraft, and is a healing tree of great virtue. It seems that the conflicting stories are due to the fact that, of all trees, the elder has a very strong feminine soul, highly individuated and advanced in consciousness. She deplores humanity's attitude to Nature and its spirits and will chastise us if not propitiated. From many parts of Europe come tales of the elder tree disengaging itself and wandering around villages at night, horrifying the populace by peeping in at lighted windows.

The elder is a deeply magical, healing and fragrant tree to grow in the garden, and it is said that certain elves attach themselves to the tree spirit, sitting beneath the elder in adoration. These elves can be called upon to grant wishes, if the supplicating human is of a humble and well-intentioned disposition.

When planting a tree in the garden in the hope that the fairies will bring it under their special protection, bear in mind that it must be positioned in a wild corner where it will be hidden from overlooking human dwellings by a natural screen comprising hedging or companion trees. However, the fairy tree itself must be set a little apart, because a fairy tree is always a lone tree. Plant it at one of the fairy hours and on one of the fairy days (see page 31), asking the fairies to adopt it and protect it as you do so. Renew this request at the special fairy hour each day for nine successive days. Although tree-planting is best done in early spring and autumn, the fairy tree will need to be garlanded with ragwort crowns and wreaths in order to encourage the fairy blessing. The golden-flowered ragwort may be gathered on Midsummer's Eve at the accustomed fairy hour, and the garlands made up to be hung on the branches of the fairy tree with due ceremony on Midsummer's Day.

FAIRY TREE MEDITATION

(To be performed beneath the boughs of the fairy tree) Think on these things . . .

. . . that trees are the largest living beings on earth . . . that trees form crowns which their trunks can support, linking our own spiritual structure comprising the higher and lower mind, or the heavenly and earthly nature, with theirs . . . that their sturdy wood-making propensities make them a symbol of our evolving souls as the tree 'reincarnates' year by year and adds to the building and ultimate perfection of its 'temple' . . . that the trees grow in majestic silence, in perfect harmony with their environment – if such power was manufactured by us we would create masses of pollution and noise in producing it . . . that the trees possess guardian spirits which can heal through a magical process, spirit responding to spirit, and that they have medicinal properties which orthodox medicine can use; they emanate soothing energies and can absorb our pain, confusion and distress . . . that trees are the exorcists of the Earth, imprisoning and disempowering malignant spirits . . . that trees receive spiritual knowledge in the form of transmitted vibrations from stars which are helping humanity and the Earth to evolve; trees 'translate' these energies into a vibrational 'language' that we can understand and then feed it into the thought sphere of the planet, where it is received and understood by properly evolved and attuned souls . . . that trees often embrace a ritual and sacrificial death, accepting the death-yielding blow of the lightning because at the moment of their demise, whether by burning or uprooting, they are able to absorb huge quantities of destructive energy lurking in the surrounding area and release it again as a positive charge; this kind of death, to which the tree willingly submits, is only one of a number of forms of sacrifice which trees embrace for the good and the progress of humanity; they richly deserve our love, friendship and veneration.

A study for *Daydream*, Dante Gabriel Rossetti, 1828-82

Flowers and the Feminine Spirit

The magical teachings of the Goddess can come to us through the medium of flowers. The great Earth Angel, working with the forces of Nature and served by diligent workers from all the four elements, channels the wisdom and inspiration of the Divine Mother, Queen of Heaven and Earth, and the result of this spiritual outpouring manifests itself continuously in the natural world about us.

We can learn much simply by our soul response to flowers. Through contemplation of their beauty and meditation upon their form, hue and fragrance, carried out with spiritually attuned sensitivity and receptivity, a gradual unfolding of their mysteries and the instruction they offer for the development of our souls will quietly come into being.

We must also study the myths and folklore surrounding flowers so that our deeper insight may fully awaken into the sunshine of Divine Mother's wisdom, and our inner eye behold the exquisitely subtle detail without an understanding of which we would fail to appreciate the fabulous tapestry of physical and spiritual life which she weaves to sustain our growth and progress. Myth and folklore arise from an intuitive and imaginative perception of spiritual reality or truth. It is this rendering of truth which we must seek in the folk tale, confident that its intuitive wisdom springs from that sacred Source which enshrines the eternal feminine principle, the heart of the Goddess.

Speak not – whisper not;
Here blowest thyme and bergamot;
Softly on the evening hour
Sweet herbs their spices shower.
(Walter De La Mare)

FLOWER HEALING

Many flowers, herbs and trees also have healing properties – perhaps all have some, waiting to be discovered. As you create your own enchanted garden, the flowers you grow will be particularly blessed, and it will be well to use these in salads or as tisanes (herbal teas) for health and healing. Of course, flowers should never in any circumstances be eaten or infused until you have ascertained their species, variety and whether or not they are safe to consume. Enchanter's nightshade (*Circaea lutetiana*) is very poisonous, for instance, as is monkshood (*Aconitum napellus*) and henbane (*Hyoscyanus niger*), and even the graceful foxglove (*Digitalis purpurea*) must be treated with caution as it can sometimes cause a

The Colours and Fragrances of Early Summer, Benjamin Perkins

kind of temporary madness. Consult a reliable herbal to learn the healing virtues of the flowers of your choice, and put yourself in a doctor's care so that he or she can monitor your illness. In this way, you can feel safe and confident in your dealings with herbs, for they have much gentle solace and healing to offer distressed and ailing humankind.

The general rule of thumb for tisanes is one heaped teaspoonful of the fresh herb (flowers and leaves) infused for one minute only. Dried herbs need two minutes. Tisanes should be light and pleasant to look at. This will assist in forming the habit of drinking them!

Gather the herbs in sunshine, if possible. The magical hours of three, six, nine and twelve are good times for herb gathering. Pick only clean, healthy plants in clean, healthy locations free from pesticides and other contaminants. Use a basket – plastic bags make the herbs sweat and their properties dilute; they also tend to turn black when drying. However, it should be noted that fresh herbs are always preferable to dried. Herbal teas should be taken four times each day, one cup or more at a time. The more tea you can manage to drink, the better; but if you have a heart condition, excess fluids should be avoided. If weak kidneys cause you to retain fluid, drink nettle tea mixed with horsetail. This will soon resolve the problem.

If a flower or a herb roots naturally in your garden, take note of it and enquire into its healing virtues. Cosmic vibrations resonate in harmony with you and your needs, and the flower, herb or tree that you need for your own healing (or for the balance and healing of the garden soil) will seed of its own accord; this process is enhanced and encouraged when you build an enchanted garden.

TULIP

The Persians anciently called this handsome spring flower the 'turban flower'. Tulips became immensely popular in seventeenth-century Europe; at the height of 'tulip mania' a strain called Viceroy sold at £250 for a single root, and another variety, Semper Augustus, for almost twice as much!

Folklore tells of a meadow in England which was inhabited by fairies (meaning that they kept their underground courts beneath it, and used its surface for their revels in the moonlight). In a nearby cottage lived an old woman who tended a very pretty garden, wherein grew a bed of especially lovely tulips. The fairies delighted in this spot, and would carry their infants thither, singing them to sleep with sweet lullabies. Sometimes, musical airs of such mellifluence were heard in the vicinity of the tulip bed that it seemed as if the flowers were making music of themselves. At dawn, the fairies returned from the meadow where they had been making merry, and could be heard caressing and murmuring to their infants as they carried them back to the fairy fort.

The tulips remained in bloom all summer through because of the fairy enchantment, and were as fragrant as roses. This so enraptured the old woman that she would never suffer a single flower to be plucked from its stem.

In time she died; and her successor uprooted the enchanted flowers and planted a parsley bed in their place. The fairies were so distressed that they cast a blight over the whole garden, and for many years nothing at all would grow within its confines except rank weeds. Yet the fairies tended the old woman's grave so that the grass which grew over it was ever bright green, and the loveliest flowers disported themselves wantonly among its blades, although no human hand ever planted or sowed or in any way ministered to the grave.

This story seems to suggest that, where human insensitivity does not recognize the presence of love and the harmony and beauty that are its gifts and its manifestation, the life forces wither away, withdrawing to and remaining with the source of that love. A salutary lesson, perhaps, in our ecologically troubled times!

LAVENDER

One of the loveliest and most evocative of all flower scents, lavender has sometimes been called the good witch's herb because of its soothing and restorative properties and its more magical qualities of protection and purification. Evil spirits quail at the aroma of lavender, and all malicious spells and ill-wishing are cleansed and rendered harmless by its beneficent presence.

Lavender is efficacious in promoting the state of mind required for meditation and for contacting one's own soul; perhaps for this reason the Romans would perfume their baths with its leaves and flowers. Butterflies and bees love this herb, and the proud rose, disdainful of so many flowers, takes pleasure in the proximity of lavender.

Lavender is associated with love, romance and remembrance, because its fragrance is everlasting. It was a perfume beloved of kings, in particular King Henry III of England and Charles VI of France. The Abbess Hildegarde, a twelfth-century visionary and healer, favoured this plant and extolled its virtues.

Lavender was chief among the herbs dedicated to Hecate, goddess of witches and sorcerers, and to her two daughters, Medea the child-murderer and Circe the moon goddess. (Although Circe was a moon goddess by virtue of being Hecate's daughter, she was also a 'daughter of Helios' or the sun.) Thus does lavender's folklore bid us remember the purging and healing qualities of darkness, and that evil is present in our world to be transformed and transmuted, representing as it does the negative terminal of the battery of life. The Goddess teaches that the deeper purpose of evil is within the perfect scheme of the Godhead and will eventually, through the alchemy of human experience on Earth, vivify and add unto the stores of what is beautiful and good . . . and so lavender, herb of Hecate and her sinister daughter, shines forth with bright Circe her sister and averts the Evil Eye.

Use lavender to drive away coughs and nervous headaches. As a mouthwash, it improves the gums and banishes halitosis. It cures night sweats and muscle stiffness. It acts as a gentle anti-depressant and will banish nervous debility and stress.

LILY

This regal flower is the symbol of purity. Its mystic number is six, the sign of the human spirit perfectly aligned with Heaven and ascending into it while the heavenly consciousness forms a downward-pointing triangle, focusing the rarefied spiritual influences into a single point, the waiting soul of humanity whose true home is the human heart. Thus we have the six-pointed star, the earthly and the heavenly triangles interpenetrating in absolute unity, creating an unceasing and undimming outpouring of divine light, *fiat lux*. This is the one real goal of human life on Earth, and is why the lily appears again and again in religious and mystic paintings and works of art down the ages of man. When in such paintings the lily appears in conjunction with

White Roses and Lavender, Benjamin Perkins

the Madonna it is to indicate that the Virgin's soul was aspiring heavenwards, concentrated entirely on the purity of spirit and freed from the imbalance of 'good' and 'evil'. The lily makes only a tenuous root, feeding itself from its bulb, its own source, as though its flower were truly a gift from Heaven.

Folklore tells of lilies, unplanted by any human hand, appearing spontaneously on the graves of those executed for crimes they did not commit. This seems to indicate that such poor souls were able to forgive earthly brutality, ignorance and injustice and ascend to Heaven without entanglement on the lower astral planes. Ghost stories both ancient and modern consistently report that those who are executed for their crimes remain very close to the Earth in an agonized state after their bodily death, where in their confusion and desperation they incite others still on Earth whose souls have been opened to darkness to commit further terrible crimes. The gentle and loving influence of the lily, sweetly angelic, comes to give aid to such suffering human souls, inspiring them to make a huge effort of forgiveness and so to cast off and rise above the snares of their emotional torment.

The lily is also a signature of feminine sexuality. Folklore teaches that if a man tramples upon a lily, he destroys the purity of his womenfolk. This, adjusted a little out of the focus of conventional interpretation, is actually a feminist statement. When the male principle tramples underfoot the feminine principle, either within himself or within his community, then the female essence is hurt and even destroyed. Wisewomen of ancient tribes and ancient lineage tell us that women today are partly in shadow, and that our true powers and dignity must rise again before we can throw off this 'trampling' that has been perpetrated against us.

The fecundity of the Madonna and of the Earth are one, so it is said that when Madonna lilies are plentiful, crops of corn will follow suit and bread will be cheap. Folklore also informs us that the lily keeps away ghosts and that the presence of the flower in the garden will ensure protection from such dubious visitors; but as we have already seen, this service of the lily needs to be interpreted in the light of its merciful healing properties for the soul, because it gently bids arisen souls (which when they are entrapped in the astral regions

Convent Thoughts, Charles Allston Collins, 1828-73

Lilies of all kinds. Shakespeare, *The Winter's Tale*

surrounding Earth we call 'ghosts') to unloose their fetters and to press onwards into the spiritual worlds. Such is the message of the lily.

LILY OF THE VALLEY

An old country name for this charming flower is Liriconfancy. Because all white, sweet-scented flowers are associated with the soul, it was a natural progression for simple rural folk to associate them with death, and so tradition advises against planting out a bed of lilies of the valley which is exclusive to the flower alone – other flowers must grow among them.

Again, this lily is a flower of the Virgin – it is said that these flowers first sprang up where her tears fell to the ground as she experienced the bitterness of her Seven Sorrows; and so another name for them is Our Lady's Tears. Another legend tells us that they first bloomed where St Leonard's blood fell during his battle of three days with the dragon. Esoterically, the dragon is the lower mind, the earthly nature; it is with this that each one of us must struggle and finally conquer before we can attain spiritual mastery.

Lily of the valley reduces high blood pressure and cures dropsical conditions. Patients recovering from symptoms inflicted by strokes will find it helpful. It may be used to treat heart failure and difficulty with breathing due to congestive conditions of the heart.

NASTURTIUM

This fiery-coloured flower of the sun has its origins in the tropics. The Tropic of Cancer and the Tropic of Capricorn represent the polarities of winter and summer, astrologically speaking, and in esotericism the polarities of darkness and light, which form the point of balance at their point of intersection. This point of balance between the forces of light and of darkness is truly to be found in the human heart; therein is the magical node of power which, when fully understood, will give us mastery over the external world because we have achieved veritable mastery within. This will have nothing to do with conquering or suppressing Nature, but rather with summoning and exalting her powers because we have honoured and embraced her

Lilies of the Valley, Benjamin Perkins

Sweet is the lore which Nature brings.
Wordsworth, *The Tables Turned*

from within. We will be married to Nature because we will find that there is no separation between her and the human spirit. The external world maps truth out for us in signs and symbols, and it is important to dwell on these mysteries that the tropics demonstrate when we consider the nasturtium.

The nasturtium radiates a tremendous psychic force of heat and light. As a plant of the sun, its colours are all yang in tone, bright and vivid. Its seeds, eaten in salads, bring a balance of yin and yang to the diet.

At the beginning of the century, a Sun Brotherhood came together in Holland. It was part of the spiritual wave which earlier had borne the Romantic Poets on its crest and afterwards had given rise to the intensity of artistic creation in France and the Pre-Raphaelite Brotherhood in England. This Sun Brotherhood came together to live in Bohemian wooden huts surrounded by gardens strewn with a wilderness of nasturtium, burgeoning in the fences and hedges and clasping fruit trees in its colourful embrace. The nasturtium belonged to this community as a soul force in Nature which expressed the spiritual sublimity and emotional intensity of the Brotherhood. They lived for art and the simplicity and loveliness of life.

The hot mustard oil nasturtium produces may be used as an antibiotic on malignant bacteria and moulds. To disinfect the mouth and the throat, chew one or two nasturtium leaves. The plant may be used in conjunction with butterbur (a plant similar to coltsfoot but much larger, with leaves as big as hats and burrs with formidable adhesive qualities) to cure emphysema of the lungs. Nasturtium also improves the sight.

MEADOWSWEET

In the *Mabinogion*, a magical history of ancient Celtic Wales, Gwydyon, son of the Mother Goddess Dôn, is a Merlinesque figure and has as his faithful companion Dôn's own grandson Lleu, the Shining One. Gwydyon decides to make a bride of flowers for Lleu because the boy's mother has put a curse on him to the effect that he can take no wife of the race of men upon the Earth. So Lleu and Gwydyon use their 'magic and enchantments and conjure a woman out of flowers'. They name her Blodeuedd ('flowers').

This woman of flowers is created from the flowers of oak and broom and meadowsweet and reveals meadowsweet as a fairy plant.

Queen Elizabeth I, who delighted in fairy lore, always kept the floors of her apartments strewn with meadowsweet flowers.

Meadowsweet quickly soothes an upset stomach. It may be used in all cases of enteritis and diarrhoea. It will also help to cure high blood pressure, diabetes and disorders of the blood, and will reduce fever and ease the pain of rheumatism.

COWSLIP

A strange story of the Lincolnshire fens concerns the uniting of a human soul with the spirit of the flower known as the cowslip or, as country people call it, the 'keys of heaven'.

One wintertime the daughter of a family who lived in a village in the fens fell ill, and although everything was done to preserve her life, it soon became clear that she would die. Her family's best hope was that she would live to see the spring, which had always been her favourite time of year; yet the cold, dreary days passed with no sign of any seasonal change, although it was already April. The stricken parents thought their daughter must die before greeting the spring, and their distress was all the deeper. At last, when her spirit seemed to be on the point of departing, the girl said to her mother, 'If the Green Mist [a supernatural phenomenon which indicated that spring had arrived] does not come tomorrow, I can stay no longer. The earth is calling me and the seeds are bursting that will cover me, but if I could only live as long as one of those cowslips that grow by the door each spring, I swear I'd be content.'

Her mother hushed her, for the air was full of listeners in those days; but the next day the Green Mist came, and the girl sat in the sun and was filled with joy and laughter. As the spring days went by, she grew stronger and prettier with every one, unless it happened to be a cold and sunless day when it seemed winter had returned; then her strength failed and she became pale as death. When the cowslips flowered she grew so strangely lovely that her beauty almost made her family afraid. She warned them not to gather any of the cowslips, and they were careful to obey; but one day a lad came to the cottage who plucked one of the flowers and played with it as he chatted to the family. The girl did not see what he had done until he said goodbye, when she saw the cowslip lying on the earth. 'Did thee pull that cowslip?' she asked, putting her hand to her head.

'Aye,' he replied, bending and presenting it to her, and marvelling at her beauty.

She accepted the flower and stood looking about her in the garden. She gave a sudden cry and ran into the house. Her family found her prostrate on her bed, clasping the frail cowslip to her breast. All day long she faded and in the morning her mother found her lying dead and withered like the expired flower in her hand.

This story (believed to be true among the people of the fens) points to the marvellous spiritual connection our own souls share with flowers, and indeed with all Nature . . . truly we are not separate from any of her forms or the consciousness they contain.

Cowslip gives protection from strokes, helps bronchial conditions, comforts the victims of colds and chills, soothes pain and calms the nerves. It charms away nervous exhaustion and ensures a restful night's sleep. The leaves, in a cold-cream base, discourage wrinkles.

A close cousin of the cowslip, the oxlip is a woodland flower with soporific qualities which can give visions and second sight or 'fairy sight'. Shakespeare, well versed in fairy lore and, it seems, gifted with the fairy sight, mentions oxlips in connection with the Fairy Queen:

> I know a bank where the wild thyme blows,
> Where oxlips and the nodding violet grows,
> Quite overcanopied with luscious woodbine,
> With sweet musk-roses and with eglantine.
> There sleeps Titania sometime of the night,
> Lulled in these flowers with dances and delight . . .

PASSION FLOWER

Christ represented within his own being the child of the marriage of the God and Goddess, employing the active masculine principle yet expressing the secret wisdom of the heart which the Goddess enshrines. From this sacred marriage springs love-in-action, the Christ principle itself, perfectly realized in the spirit and the life of Jesus Christ. The 'passion' flower is a token of his passion – that is, his redemption of unenlightened humanity through the gift of his

Oxlips, Benjamin Perkins

Benjamin Perkins

supreme suffering and sacrifice. This is how the passion flower externalizes the Christ mystery: the leaf is an emblem of the spear which pierced Christ's side; the five anthers symbolize the five wounds; the tendrils, the cords or whips; the column of the ovary, the pillar of the cross; the stamens, the hammers; the three styles, the three nails; the fleshy threads within the flowers, the crown of thorns; the calyx, the glory or nimbus; the white tint, purity; the blue tint, Heaven; the strange and delightful perfume, the incense of earthly atoms transmuting to spiritual atoms in the resurrection; it remains open for three days, signifying the three years' ministry of Christ.

Passion flower may be used to treat chronic insomnia, and its oil, taken orally, benefits the skin. It soothes neuralgia and shingles, and helps asthma patients. As an anti-spasmodic, it helps in cases of Parkinson's disease, seizures and hysteria.

PANSY

Allegedly struck by Cupid's dart, the pansy has often been used in love-philtres. It fortifies the heart, and has excellent anti-convulsive and sedative properties, so it may be used to stop repeated vomiting and to ensure restful sleep. It helps cases of heart failure, chronic asthma, catarrh and epilepsy.

POPPY

The flower of sleep and sweet forgetfulness, the poppy is the true corn flower. An ancient Greek legend relates how the poppy was conjured by Somnus, God of Sleep, to give to Ceres, the Corn Goddess, when she was so exhausted by the search for her lost daughter that she became unable to make the corn grow. To save humanity from famine, Somnus brought her poppies to compel her to fall asleep. The poppies' magic stole her away into slumber, where she visited the halls of wisdom in the celestial world and awoke strengthened and comforted, able to resume her divine mission of ministering to the corn. It was therefore believed in ancient times that it was essential to the welfare of the corn that poppies should flourish among it. Is this old story a mythic drama which depicts in images the essential unity of the body (corn) and the spirit (the sleep-inducing poppy) and shows that we should never forget the significance of the spirit as our true source in our joy and diligence in meeting the needs of the body? Certainly it would seem so.

Strangely, this symbolism of the poppy as a token of remembrance has acquired a new aspect in modern times because of its uncanny appearance in great numbers just before and during the two World Wars on the English coast, where 'Poppy-Land' came into being and was the celebrated meeting-place of poets, artists and thinkers, and because of its growth on the devastated fields of Flanders, where we may hope it brought 'sleep and sweet forgetfulness' to that anguished place. The poppy is of course famous in our own era as the official flower of Remembrance Day; that it brought solace to a parent grieving over a lost child in mythology is a demonstration of the consistency existing between the earthly and the sublime worlds.

The red poppy will relieve persistent coughs and clear respiratory catarrh. The milky juice obtained from the seed-head has narcotic properties. Inflamed throats and chests respond well to the poppy tisane, which also cures catarrh, hay fever, asthma and general respiratory illnesses.

ROSE

The sign of the rose is really a double symbol. Its structure, formed from a calyx of five sepals, makes the shape of a pentagram. Five is the number of humanity, for if we stand with our arms slightly raised and our feet slightly spread we form the same figure. Five is a magical sign, the number of the five bodily senses and the number of Christ's wounds on the cross, signifying that it is through suffering in an earthly body that we will gain liberation from the bonds of matter. Yet the rose is also the sign of the heart, numerologically given as six. While the lily signifies angelic purity, the rose is a living sigil for the human being. Rooted in clay, enclosed in a physical body, we are nourished by the magical darkness of Earth so that we may become co-creators with the Godhead, a golden promise more precious even than the heritage of the angels, whose flower is the lily. Therefore the number of the rose is both five and six, making eleven, the sign of the double one standing side by side, 11, God and his-her co-creator, humanity. This is why the rose and the lily appear together in religious and mystic paintings, and why the rose, even above the lily, is revered and venerated as the Queen of Flowers and the Keeper of

Mysteries. The rose cherishes a secret of great price in its heart like a jewel (*sub rosa*). It is the secret of human happiness and perfect fulfilment which lies in the balance that the mysteries of the human heart can achieve, for the polarities of the universal life forces meet in the heart. Only Love, the divine flame of spirit alive and leaping in the human heart, can create this miraculous balance, which when achieved will give all things their true nature, glorious and of God, chasing away the shadows of evil and suffering. The seasonal cycle represents the state of this imbalance, so that there is alternately warmth and cold, being and non-being, plenty and want, a time of flowers and beauty succeeded by a barren and desolate aftermath, the 'flowers' and the 'thorns' of the mystical rose.

Originally all roses were white, conjured into being when the goddess Venus (or Aphrodite) rose from the sea, so that they might clothe her naked body. When Venus ran in anguish to her lover Adonis, who had been wounded, she tore her flesh upon the thorn of a rose and her blood fell upon the flower, giving birth to the red rose. So it was the pangs of love, the passion of the Christ, the suffering of humanity which brought forth the red rose. This story is beautifully reworked in Oscar Wilde's fairytale 'The Nightingale and the Rose'.

Use the flowers of the rose as a miraculous tonic for the heart and brain. The wild rose is best, but the garden varieties, especially the white rose, will have a similar effect. The rose is a panacea and will successfully treat a wide variety of disorders, including stomach problems, female ailments, catarrh, kidney and bladder disease, gall-bladder, constipation, exhaustion and skin problems. If you cannot find a herb to treat your illness, try the efficacious rose!

SNOWDROP

The snowdrop, like the lily of the valley, is a holy flower. Similarly white and with bowed head, it is an eternal symbol of hope, brought from Eden by an angel to the banished and desolate Eve. Snow was falling fast, and all was dark, barren, freezing and lifeless. The Angel of Sorrow, come to bring consolation, promised Eve and her consort that even in this terrible exile in the world beyond Eden, spring would follow the pitiless winter. He breathed upon some of the

Snowdrops, Benjamin Perkins

falling snowflakes, and on touching the ground they were transformed into snowdrops, which ever since have brought hope and comfort and the promise of spring in the darkest winter days. Another name for this demure little flower is 'fair maid of February'.

Prepare an ointment from the crushed bulbs in a castor-oil base for the treatment of chilblains, frostbite and rough skin caused by the frost. This can also be beneficially applied to the eyes.

ROSEMARY

Rosemary is a tonic for the heart and the liver, and heals digestive troubles and menstrual cramps. It calms nerves, banishes exhaustion and helps to regulate the blood pressure. The aroma protects from troubled dreams and anxiety, and a lotion made from rosemary cures head pains. Rosemary tisane with honey will cause a cough to subside, and the same mixture will keep wrinkles at bay. Rosemary benefits the skin, hair and scalp, so it is a good idea to keep a jug of the tisane for use in the bathroom.

PRIMROSE

The primrose relieves insomnia and stress, and soothes the pain of rheumatism and arthritis.

MARIGOLD

Marigold is a cleansing herb, and its tisane has been known to cure cancer. It will heal internal and external ulcers and open sores. It will also fight mucous successfully, and clears varicose veins and other circulatory problems. An infusion of the petals applied as a lotion will balance the oil production of the skin.

HEATHER

Heathers help exhausted nerves to recuperate and will restore depressed spirits. Heather is the convalescent's herb, and taken early in the spring will help us to shake off the winter blues.

Midsummer Eve, Edward Robert Hughes, 1851-1914

VIOLET

The violet has strong dissolvent qualities and can eliminate bladder and kidney 'stones' and 'gravel'. A poultice made of the pulped leaves may be applied to tumours, goitres, boils and swollen glands while the patient also takes the tisane. Violets still the nerves and will cure a congested chest. They fortify the heart and are especially good for angina pectoris. Violet leaves in a tisane cure headaches, and the leaves and flowers together stimulate the intellect and heal pleurisy.

COMPANION PLANTING

It is important to remember that plants reflect the human soul, that feminine aspect of the totality of the human spirit. The soul is essentially feminine because it wields the yin power of receptivity. Flowers symbolize the Taoist principle of Wu Wei, the Goddess force which overcomes by yielding. This universal and supremely powerful energy expresses itself sweetly, gently and beautifully in the ideation of flowers. They are perfect signatures of the heavenly consciousness, in manifestation on Earth by virtue of the Mother Goddess's ability to receive such consciousness into herself and give it forth again at the earthly level, clothed in new forms but perfect in principle. Without this nurturing, receptive force, there would be no life, no coming into being.

As expressions of the soul energy, flowers and trees have aspirations, sympathies, antipathies and dynamics of their own, and it is these we must learn if we are to build a peaceful community of flowers in the enchanted garden.

Roses are dignified souls which demand space around them so that they may perfect their self-expression. However, they love sharply aromatic plants and will gladly tolerate the presence of onions, garlic, lavender, thyme and rosemary. They deeply dislike carnations and mignonettes, although they can resign themselves to lupins, parsley and marigolds.

The daffodil and the tulip do not do well together; lilac also dislikes the tulip, although it likes lupins. Again, lupins are the only

Violets, Benjamin Perkins

violets dim,
But sweeter than the lids of Juno's eyes
Or Cytherea's breath.
Shakespeare, *The Winter's Tale*

flowers that will thrive near lily of the valley, as other flowers do not like them.

Poppies, monkshood and rue are unwilling to allow other flowers to flourish, so give them space and seclusion. Fennel starves other plants in its vicinity, so it is better to cultivate this herb in a generous-sized pot to avoid difficulties. Wormwood, lemon balm and coriander hurt fennel in their turn.

Avoid growing a vine near the cabbage patch, although the cabbages will welcome the presence of camomile. The bay tree also dislikes the vine, but the vine enjoys the close company of elms, poplars and poppies. The oak disdains the olive and the walnut tree, but the olive loves the fig tree, the maple and the myrtle. Hawthorn likes lilac and elder but is positively distressed by the presence of the blackthorn.

The birch and the fir court one another, but the birch keeps the oak at a distance. Lavender dries up cucumber, but the vegetable remains juicy and succulent if planted near horseradish and other hot plants. Radishes and spring onions fail if planted near to one another, although other types of onion fare well with radishes. Potatoes are fond of marigolds, lupins, broad beans, nasturtiums, cabbages, sweet corn and peas.

Strawberries like borage, lettuce and spinach, but cannot bear gladioli anywhere near them, and in fact if these flowers are present in a garden where strawberries are cultivated, even a long way off, the flavour of the fruit will be diminished.

Beans do not like onions or beetroot, but they courteously welcome the presence of cabbage, cauliflower, celery, leeks, sweet corn and carrots. Yarrow, marigolds, lupins and foxgloves are loved by all the garden. Cornflowers and violets are good friends. Tomatoes like asparagus and parsley but dislike potatoes and apricot trees.

A clove of garlic grown beside each rose bush will keep away pests and, if prevented from flowering, will enhance the perfume of the roses. Plant sage, hyssop and mint to keep caterpillars off vegetables, herbs and flowers. Nasturtiums will chase off woolly aphids, whitefly and the spider mite if their tendrils are allowed to twine around fruit trees. Apple trees in particular produce tastier crops if foxgloves, wallflowers and lupins are grown in their vicinity. Sawdust and oak leaves will banish slugs – if they are persistent, a dish of beer will end their lives painlessly and blissfully! Fern leaves scattered in the bed will drive off the strawberry weevil, and pine needles will improve the flavour of the strawberries. Rosemary keeps at bay the carrot fly, and mint grown between vegetables discourages many different pests.

Moles are deterred by peeled garlic bulbs placed in their holes. It is also an old country custom to write a letter to the mole and ask it to move off!

Mice are repelled by the leaves of the everlasting pea, and foxes hate vinegar, although plenty must be used to keep them at bay.

GARDENING LORE

Here are a few pieces of ancient advice which will enhance the beauty and fertility of your garden. For a profusion of sweet flowers, bury banana skins and copious amounts of fat (one pound for each bush) around the roots of rose bushes each year in the early spring.

Change the sites of your herbs, replacing a 'hot' herb such as thyme with a 'cool' herb such as mallow each year, for this encourages hardy growth and a rich, sweet aroma.

An infusion of horsetail and stinging nettle will gently cleanse your plants of aphids and other pests, and rotted nettles make a good green manure.

Collect windings of hair from your hairbrush and lay them at the bottom of planting holes or channels for trees, shrubs and flowers. The hair deters insects and moles from attacking their roots before they are established.

Bury old leather boots and shoes deep in the soil before planting out new beds. The nutrients from the slowly rotting leather will enrich the soil. Pour ale over hollyhocks, lupins and foxgloves to keep them in flower and to enhance their colours.

SOLOMON'S MAGIC RING

It is said that King Solomon possessed a marvellous ring which enabled him to speak to the birds of the skies and the creatures of the Earth. This 'magic ring' is a ring of faith, composed of spiritual light. You can create it as a magical seal for yourself if you will be kind and gentle towards our animal and insect brethren.

Create a little altar upon which you will place sweet-scented white flowers, and light a white, a green and a brown candle at ten o'clock in the evening, which is Gabriel's hour. It must be the night of the new moon, and you must bow reverently to the Angel of the Moon (mighty Gabriel) before proceeding. If you can manage to have the mysterious green stone known as aventurine close at hand, and in addition a sapphire (the 'seal of secrets'), that is all the better. Speak this charm:

King Solomon, King Solomon, I seek thy hallowed ring;
So I may talk with the beasts, and hear what the birds sing.

Now call upon the Angels of Glory, the four called Chasan, Arel, Phorlakh and Talishad, to help you in your creative endeavours. Some souls call in simplicity upon the Angels of Love and Light for their blessing. Only remember this is a working which must flow forth in purity from the heart. Call also upon the Great God Pan to lead you into his magic kingdom, for he is a benign Nature spirit.

Say the charm three times over, pausing between each declaration to visualize your inmost heart drawing close to that majestic being in the supernal worlds who is the soul essence of the animal kingdom. When we bless animals with human love, we stimulate the heart centre of this ineffable being and move nearer to achieving worldwide harmony with our animal brethren. The sanctuary of a loved and tended garden is the perfect place to seek communion with animals and birds; and even if you work the spell indoors, it is better to choose a situation where a window overlooks the garden.

As the charm is spoken for the last time, imagine that the Archangel Gabriel bestows Solomon's ring on you as a gift from the spirit. The ring will be placed on the third finger of your left hand.

Repeat the ceremony once again at full moon, and a third time upon the night of the next new moon, and the task is done. You will at once begin to understand what birds and animals are thinking and feeling, and will start to enter into natural meditations with them whereby your own thoughts are channelled to them and exchanged with theirs. The love you radiate towards birds and animals, your kindness and gentleness in your dealings with them, will ensure that the wearing of Solomon's charmed ring is a lifelong gift.

Astarte Syriaca, Dante Gabriel Rossetti, 1828-82

STARCRAFT IN THE GARDEN AND
THE SEAT OF LEARNING

Every garden devoted to the awakening of spiritual consciousness and the unfolding of soul perception should have a seat of learning. A simple stone or wooden bench will suffice, but when sitting for meditation it is essential to be comfortable, so cushions or a seat pad will be necessary. Ideally, your seat of learning should be south-facing, partially shaded and set in a private nook. If you have a pond in the garden, set your seat nearby, for still, reflective water is a symbol of the soul.

Sitting on this seat of learning, in a relaxed pose with spine erect to facilitate meditation, you can contact the fairies and the Angel of the Garden for direct, precise and practical advice about siting plants, the particular needs of your flowers and trees, and how to tackle their problems when they show signs of disease or dispiritedness. You may, for instance, have planted a tree or a shrub where the earth is disturbed by geopathic stress, so the plant will need to be moved and the area healed by growing the pretty wild strawberry over the area for some years.

Information from the Angel and the fairies will be channelled to you in such a way that their inspiration will be received as the direct prompting of your own thoughts. Saint Dorothea, the saint of the garden, will also guide and bless your endeavours and offer you resolutions to problems; it is simply a matter of attuning, building your half of the bridge through meditation and inner stillness.

Practise the presence of the Goddess in the garden, which means identifying your soul with hers, experiencing the magic of her consciousness in your own heart, letting her descend into you so that you see with her tender gaze, her serenity, the power of her love and blessing. The enchanted garden is a reflection of Eden where the gardener can walk with angels, speak with the Great Spirit and commune with arisen souls. As you use the garden in this way, so you will become aware of many precious secrets – the magical dimensions of the sky above the garden and the earth below it, the marvels of matter and the singing, seeing life in the stones (rocks have been

The Child Enthroned (detail), Thomas Cooper Gotch,
1854-1931

discovered which, when struck, can play the complete diatonic scale), the mystical connection between bird life and the consciousness of angels and how their evolution is interlinked, how fragrant flowers are reflections of our own souls and will give us creative dreams for making our garden more beautiful, ever more a receptacle for spiritual radiance.

Contemplate the grandeur of the treasury of stars which shine over the garden. You can vivify and charm your garden with the light of the stars so that it does indeed become a healing sanctuary. This 'starcraft' is the simple act of absorbing their starlight into the soul (located at the heart centre) and giving it out again into the heart of the garden. This mystical heart of the garden is linked with your own and you will intuitively know where it is. The absorption and exhalation of this 'star fire' is a magical expression of love in action. It is an act of will directed by love, occurring in the imagination, the soul or heart mind, not the frontal mind of the uncreative intellect.

As we look out upon the vast universe, it is good to reflect that that great firmament of all life is itself an enchanted cosmic garden, for the energy centres of the Solar Logos are forever manifesting in the form of mighty lotus flowers, complete with their jewel centres, their golden stamens, in which lies hidden that central core which is esoterically called the Planetary Logos, the source of the mystery of human evolution. It is from these rapturously beautiful lotus-flower centres that the Godhead broadcasts the forces which make up life, and there is a reciprocal action between stars, trees and humanity, unknown to us as yet, which relays, receives and interprets these divine commands. All creation takes place in an enchanted garden, and one day we will realize the full measure of the beauty which is secreted at the heart of this poetic and literal truth.

THE WOMAN IN THE MOON

The magical moon has always been associated with the Madonna, with the tides of fecundity here on Earth, with the swelling waters and our life of the psyche which they symbolize, with everything that reflects and suggests the power of woman, spirit of wisdom. In ancient days she represented the Goddess; as feminine magic was denied, repressed and buried, she became the emblem of the feared witch; yet always she has spun a charmed circle in her orbit of the Earth which has ever resonated with romance and mystery. Many sacred groves, many divine wells, many secret hidden caves, many steadfast and silent stone circles standing age upon age, bear testimony to the ancient and mystical powers of the moon and the dynamic rites practised in her name; and yet we must think of the spiritual presence of the moon, the Goddess and the angels which signify her deeper being.

How do these mysteries relate to our practical care and shaping of the enchanted garden? We may meditate under the moon in the sanctuary and peace of our garden and learn much that cannot be mundanely expressed about the origin of our spirit and the home of our soul. Yet, apart from these mystic contemplations, the 'woman in the moon' would have us take note of her nightly meanderings, for the sake of the garden and the life that it sustains.

Here is some ancient gardening advice from the Victorian manuscripts of Sarah Greaves:

The moon traces her path through the zodiac once each month (but it is the mystic zodiac envisioned by the soul of which I speak, that magic circle which crowns the firmament just above the Earth, and not the constellations). She is the mistress of physical form, of bodies, and her creative powers are drawn from the magical influences of the stars and planets, and from the inspiration of the particular sign of the zodiac through which she is passing.

The moon especially is queen of the ocean, of bodies of water, and her waxing and waning must be taken account of by the wise gardener. Harvest your vegetables and fruits just after the full moon, when its first diminishment is still barely visible. Let your planting be done at eventide in a waning moon, for then water will run to the roots. Sow seeds during the time of the waxing moon, one day after the new moon's crescent has smiled in the skies. Prune two days after the new moon when you wish more growth; if you desire less, prune in the wane of the moon.

Choose air and fire signs for contemplation and meditation in the garden. During air days, concentrate most particularly on communing with the spirits of the trees, the inner essence of the flowers, the fairies and the elves. Make joyful contact with the sylphs of the air, for they will keep you in good humour, and bring laughter to your heart. Stake climbers in air days, and sow flowers. Sow ramblers in Gemini, and flowers in Libra. In Aquarius, meditate upon the brotherhood of all life as it is expressed in the garden: human, soil, stones, water, trees, flowers, moon, stars, skies and the fiery sun are all one brotherhood. Feel the presence of fairies and angels within the glorious scheme of this mystic brotherhood. During Aquarius, if the weather is fine, sleep for a little beneath the boughs of a tree, and let the spirit of the tree speak to you in your dreams.

Fire days are for spell-weaving. Heal and bless your garden, and chant your runes. Sow plants in Aries so that their growth is fulsome; for burgeoning growth and height, sow in Sagittarius. Leo is often too hot, so spend these days designing and planning and discouraging little wild seedlings which are becoming rampant.

Water days are for wet work, so water well and plant at this time. Sow during the water signs, only never harvest in Pisces, for your fruits and vegetables will rot away quickly. Vegetables are best harvested in Aries, and fruit in Taurus. Harvest in the last quarter of the moon, when it is in decline, if the fruit is to be kept, for then the juices will be less than in the penultimate quarter. For sweet leaves and succulent fruit, sow on water days, but remember that anything sown or harvested in Pisces cannot be preserved.

Earth signs are for wholesome toil, for spadework and sowing, thinning and transplanting. Weed in Virgo, feed in Capricorn in a waning moon (watery Scorpio is also a good time to feed), and plant potatoes, corms and bulbs in a waning moon also, upon the earth days. Gather seed in the last quarter of the moon, in Taurus or Capricorn. Herbal sprays for pest control are best administered in Virgo (use a mixture of horsetail and nettle boiled in quantity together). Any vegetable that is hot on the tongue is best harvested in Scorpio or Leo.

Earth days are also efficacious in promoting communion with the fairies, and for this purpose I would commend to you Monday, the moon's own day, when it falls on an earth sign in the lunar zodiac. If it rains upon a water day, go out into the garden and enjoy the company of the undines, the water fairies, as they laugh and tumble in the drops. It will take the dreariness of the rain away. When you light a fire to consume garden rubbish, think of the salamanders, the fire-folk, dancing in the flames.

Isabella and the Pot of Basil, William Holman Hunt, 1827-1910

Calling a Unicorn into the Garden

This very special meditation should be worked on a warm summer's evening or at first light on a perfect summer morning. The meditation is a deep one, so it is important to feel warm and relaxed. Sit at ease, with your spine straight and your right foot placed over your left, hands cupped in your lap.

Begin to ponder the mystery of the unicorn. This creature is a native of the exalted regions of the soul. It walks alone in the high places under the stars, noble and wise, one-pointed, attuned, at one with the Great Spirit. It is a symbol of healing, of making whole, of divine integration. The unicorn is truly not of this Earth; its sacred visitations, made always in its soul body, impinge on our perception through myth, poetry, fairy tale and dream. When the unicorn steps through the doorway of our imagination, its visionary presence is like the blessing bestowed by a ministering angel, because it is a revelation of our spirit, our higher essence, our aspirant self. To be united with the divine flame of spirit which is our true self is to transcend the deepest peace and the most exquisite ecstasy our hearts can conceive of; and this unity, this hallowed meeting of self with spirit, is mirrored for us in the serene vision of the unicorn, supreme symbol of the soul.

To some, the vision is sweetly erotic; and this is because the unicorn, creature of the magical moon, symbolizes in its distinct form and essence the mystic marriage between the soul and the intellect, the feminine and the masculine spiritual principles; and so the horn of the unicorn, its 'third eye' uniting the vision of the two separate eyes and giving us the secret of the power of the triangle (unity transforming division), becomes the emblem of intelligence perfected, or spiritual consciousness.

The Light of the World, William Holman Hunt, 1827-1910

Now turn from contemplation to meditation. Your deeper self is about to receive the shining vision of the unicorn into its heart. Breathe a little more deeply and a little more slowly, and feel the enhanced magical quality of the airs of the garden as they flow around you, of the radiant inner forms of the trees and the flowers, of the perfume of the soft grass at your feet. Every blade, every leaf, every petal shares the consciousness of the Great Spirit. And now you, the seeker, are looking into the mystical heart of the garden with the eyes of the spirit.

Where is this mystical heart of the garden? You know where it is because the point of consciousness where it dwells is given to you. Look deep, deep into this mystical heart and begin to see a soul form taking shape . . . that of the bright white, lightly tripping unicorn, mighty and ancient of spirit, kindly and gentle of demeanour. You see its horn, gleaming white-golden, its white flanks shining with a pure radiance, its fathomless eyes alight with a strange glory which pierces the heart with a shaft of divine love. The unicorn recognizes you, knows you! Bathe in the thrill and the gladness of this moment, and begin to call out to the unicorn. Let it be a call from your soul to your spirit; you do not need to use words, just allow this soul call to rise up and go forth from your heart. Alerted, the unicorn raises his noble head. His rippling white mane moves in the winds of the spirit. Responding, his body poised in radiance, he takes his first steps towards you. Hold out your arms to embrace him, for you and this magical being are destined to take many spiritual journeys together, adventuring deep into the heavenly worlds.

When you are ready to return to ordinary consciousness, earth yourself by making seven sunwise rings of downward-spiralling light which will wind around your crown, brow, throat, heart, solar plexus, base (of spine) and feet chakras and come right down to Earth through the centre of this spiralling tower of light. Place the symbol of the silver cross in a circle of light on your brow, throat and heart and go on your way, knowing your unicorn will always walk with you, there to respond to your call when you next wish to meet with him in the enchanted garden, bringing with him delight, joy and guiding wisdom from the divine worlds.

When the unicorn comes into the garden in answer to the aspirant's call, the pilgrim soul has come home and the enchanted garden is a figment of heavenly reality come down to Earth.

Acknowledgements

While every attempt has been made to trace the copyright holders of the Pre-Raphaelite paintings reproduced in this book, this has not always been possible. Savitri Books therefore offer their apologies to any person or organization to whom they failed to give the proper acknowledgement and will endeavour to do so in subsequent editions.

Front of jacket: Roy Miles Gallery, London/Bridgeman Art Library. *Page 11*: by courtesy of the Fogg Art Museum, Harvard University Art Museums, Bequest of Grenville L. Winthrop. *Page 14*: Private Collection/Bridgeman Art Library. *Page 21*: Christie's, London/ Bridgeman Art Library. *Page 26*: Birmingham Museums and Art Gallery. *Pages 30, 73 and 81*: Ashmolean Museum, Oxford. *Pages 34, 59, 65, 69 and 99*: Manchester City Art Galleries/Bridgeman Art Library. *Page 42*: City of Aberdeen Art Gallery and Museums Collections. *Page 47*: Board of Trustees of the National Museums and Galleries on Merseyside – Lady Lever Art Gallery, Port Sunlight. *Page 54*: Glasgow Museums – Art Gallery & Museums, Kelvingrove. *Page 93*: Fine Art Photographic Library. *Page 101*: The Estate of Thomas Cooper Gotch/Bridgeman Art Library. *Page 105*: Laing Art Gallery, Newcastle upon Tyne (Tyne and Wear Museums). *Page 107*: by permission of the Warden and Fellows of Keble College, Oxford.

NOTE ON THE BOTANICAL PAINTINGS

The fine flower paintings reproduced in this book are the work of Benjamin Perkins – a highly respected naturalist and wildlife artist, who is the author and illustrator of several books. Most of these paintings were produced between April 1995 and March 1996 and form part of a special series of wild flower pictures commissioned by Mr David Hart. The artist and Savitri Books would like to offer him their sincere thanks for allowing some of the pictures to be reproduced in *The Enchanted Garden*.